# BRISTOL
# bOYZ
# STOMP

# BRISTOL

DOREEN M. MCGETTIGAN

# bOYZ

**THE NIGHT THAT DIVIDED A TOWN**

# STOMP

*Doreen Mc Gettigan*

## TATE PUBLISHING
### AND ENTERPRISES, LLC

Published by Tate Publishing & Enterprises, LLC
127 E. Trade Center Terrace | Mustang, Oklahoma 73064 USA
1.888.361.9473 | www.tatepublishing.com

Tate Publishing is committed to excellence in the publishing industry. The company reflects the philosophy established by the founders, based on Psalm 68:11,
*"The Lord gave the word and great was the company of those who published it."*

Published in the United States of America

ISBN: 978-1-61346-563-9
1. Biography & Autobiography / Personal Memoirs
2. Family & Relationships / Death, Grief, Bereavement
11.08.25

# DEDICATION

To Birna, who has inspired me with her unending will to keep putting one foot in front of the other and for finding a way to be Birna instead of "that" young woman who lost her husband. To my loving husband, John, who believed in me and told me every single day for eleven months: "Go work on your book." To my Aunt Renee, who listened to and supported me always, I miss you. To my parents Frank and Janice Streibig, thank you for believing in me and continuing to support me. To my kids for blessing me with a continuous parade of babies to love, and to all of my grand babies and my dear nephew Michael, you have all given me a renewed hope for the future.

# TABLE OF
# CONTENTS

Foreword                                                    9
That Night                                                 11
Seventy-Two Hours                                          19
Bristol Borough                                            29
The Past                                                   33
Leaving Bristol                                            41
Road Rage, Gang Mentality, or Just Plain Murder?          49
Trying to Grieve                                           59
The Trial Starts                                           73
First Day of Trial                                         77
Second Day of Trial                                        83
Third Day of Trial                                         91
The Defense Begins                                         95
Closing Arguments                                         101
In the Jury's Hands                                       105
Post Trial                                                123
The Sentencing                                            131
More Arrests, Please?                                     141
Tragedy Strikes Again                                     149
It's All about Me                                         157
The Baby Parade                                           169
What Was I Thinking?                                      185
The Never-Ending Story                                    191
Maybe Today?                                              201

# FOREWORD

In my work as a motivational speaker, mental health and anti-bullying advocate, I meet so many people of different ages, races, classes, belief systems, etc. I take notice to how truly unique and diverse each individual is; however, I can not help but realize how every single person I come across truly has one thing in common—his or her own story. With our hectic day-to-day lives, we sometimes miss out on the most genuine and inspiring stories, because most of the time, we do not take notice to how resilient we are as individuals.

When one brave soul, such as author Doreen McGettigan, shares *her* story of the heart shattering death of her younger brother and inspires us with her courage to spread a message of hope for a better future, we realize how one story truly can start a conversation—a conversation, that she is committed to continuing.

Doreen and I are two very different people. We come from different generations yet we share similar histories of Obsessive Compulsive Disorder, being the victim's of numerous bullies' and our very different yet equally difficult struggles to return from the darkest of places.

We, as individuals, tend to feed off of each other at times. If you are an individual with a caring heart and someone who truly wants to be inspired to start the conversation that can end violence, even if just in your own space, this book is for you. If you want to spread the message of embracing our unique human resilience, this book is for you.

If you simply want to pay it forward, this book is for you.

**—Melissa Ann Hopely**
International Motivational Speaker
Mental Health & Anti-Bullying Advocate

Where would she be going this time of night? It was after midnight, and Birna was backing out of her driveway. I got one of those horrible feelings. Was something wrong with the baby? I convinced myself it was something as simple as a late-night snack. I pulled up beside her and rolled down my window.

"David got into a fight, and I have to go to the hospital and pick him up," she said.

*Really? David in a fight?* That confused me. *David does not fight. David hates fighting.* I told her I would drive her. She got into my car. I headed to the hospital. Birna told me she had no idea what had happened, other than David went to band practice. I told her about my night out with the girls, and she told me about a special dinner she had cooked for Dave. When we were close to the hospital, she asked me where I was going. Because the band practice was in Bristol, I assumed he was at Lower Bucks hospital, which was in Bristol.

"They took him to Frankford Torresdale Hospital," she told me.

My stomach dropped. I felt like I could not breathe. My heart was beating fast. My palms were sweating. Frankford Hospital is a trauma center; it is in Northeast Philadelphia. They only take some-one there from Bristol if they are seriously hurt, and they usually go in an ambulance. I was having a full-blown panic attack and, at the same time, trying to appear calm. I did not want Birna to panic. The ride to the hospital was long. I do not know how I knew where it was; I just drove. I tried to come up with conversation to keep my mind from imagining the worst. I needed information. I asked her if she was sure it had been a fight.

"Could they have said it was an accident?"

*Yes, a car accident would make more sense. They would take him to the trauma center as a precaution.*

"No," she answered. "They said it was a fight, and it happened in Bristol."

That was what she knew.

I walked up to the desk and told the receptionist I was there to pick up David Albert. She told me there was no patient there by that name. A wave of relief came over me. I asked Birna who had called her. I was tired, it was late, and I just wanted to pick Dave up and get home.

"The police," she answered, and she was quite sure they said Frankford Torresdale. I explained this to the receptionist and asked her to check again. We sat down in the waiting area. I nervously started to dig through my purse for change. I lifted my head and saw the nurse walking toward us. She was uncomfortable; I could read her face. She did not want to tell us whatever she was on her way over to tell us. She started to speak, and her words were just spinning around in my head. Did she just tell us Dave was unresponsive, he had been beaten badly, and that he needed surgery immediately to relieve pressure on his brain because of a head injury? No, we could not see him. She told us to have a seat.

I could not think in full sentences. The words *brain surgery* kept rolling around in my head. *This is scary,* I kept thinking. It was getting difficult to remain rational. Nothing was making sense. I needed to call somebody. I called my daughter, Jill. I told her where we were and asked her if she would try to call the guy's from Dave's band and find out what happened. I also asked her to call my mother and my brothers, Frank and Nick, and my sister. Brain surgery just sounded so serious, and I was not sure how much longer I could keep it together. Even if it did turn out to be not so serious, I just thought they should know.

A nurse took Birna and me into another waiting room on the second floor. It was a large, quiet room, and there was no one else in there. Birna and I just sat there. I was afraid to speak and absolutely terrified to think. I kept imagining the nurse coming in and saying, "We have stitched him up, and you can take him home."

Family members started to arrive around three in the morning. We still had no idea what had happened. There were just voices, and then silence, and then voices. I have no idea what we were talking about. It was like one of those crazy dreams where you are straining to hear what is being said, but you really do not care.

The surgery went on all through the night. Dave had been with Joey and Anthony, his bandmates, and there was a fight. That was all we knew, and it made no sense whatsoever.

*Why is David always the one who scares me?*

Early in the morning, Dave was wheeled out of surgery. We were able to see him for a minute. It was awful. He was so bruised that I did not recognize him. The doctor explained he had suffered *several* very serious head injuries. A shunt was placed in his brain to relieve pressure. He was placed in a medically induced coma. She also explained that there where many other injuries: a shattered kidney, broken bones, and deep cuts. These would have to wait, she said, because the head injuries were extremely critical. She was not optimistic. In her opinion, David would not make it. I could not believe she came right out and said it.

She was old. Sorry, but that's what I thought. Maybe around sixty-four, she was totally gray, and her hair was a straggled mess.

*A woman brain doctor… strange,* I was thinking.

Was she in medical school, like, forty years ago? She must have been smart. I did not like her, not one bit. Her words echoed in my head. I was going numb. "He is still alive." I just kept saying that. Over and over, I was telling myself to remain calm and positive. *Everything will be just fine.* Doctor's do that. They scare you to death, and then magically, everything works out fine.

I needed to know how this happened. Who did this to my baby brother and why? I knew whatever happened, it had happened in Bristol. I knew Randy Morris, the Bristol Boro Police Detective. When I worked as the manager of the Pizza Hut delivery, I used to give him and the other cops pizzas. I called him. He had no idea Dave was in critical condition. He said there had been a fight and that he was still trying to sort out the facts. He told me he was at an arraignment and would come to the hospital when he was through.

Why didn't I question him about the arraignment? Did it have something to do with the fight? I needed to talk to Anthony and Joey. They were nowhere to be found. There was no way they did this to Dave. Or did they? They were the best of friends, they were all fathers, and they always got along. They were grown-ups. I could not think of one reason they would want to beat Dave up. I did not really think that was the answer, but they were the ones who were with him. And where were they now? What was I supposed to think? Their best friend was lying in a hospital bed fighting for his life, and not even a phone call came from them.

I went into David's room. We had to take turns. A machine breathed for him. There were wires hanging and that awful *beep, beep* sound of monitors. I told him I loved him and that I would never leave him. He was covered in dry, crusty blood. I wanted to wash it off of him. The nurse said that was not a good idea right then. She explained that it was important for his brain to rest. He had pieces of glass stuck in his face and on his hands. I found that strange. Why had they not removed that glass from him? It must hurt. How did he get glass all over him? Was he in a car accident? A car accident most certainly made more sense. There had to be some confusion here. My mind was wrapped around the idea of a car accident.

I wanted my son. He was away at army boot camp. David was his best friend. My heart sank. I did not want to give him this news, but I needed him. I called the Red Cross. The woman told me she would have to speak to David's doctor. I thought, *Does she really think I would make something like this up?*

I gave her the phone number for the hospital. It felt good to be thinking of something else, to be working on something. After speaking with the doctor, the woman from the Red Cross told me they would indeed arrange to have Jimmy sent home.

*This is really bad,* I thought. *If they are sending Jimmy home from the army, it is bad.* I did not know what else to do. I was so tired. I thought of my job. It was still early, but I thought I better call my boss. I worked in advertising at the Bucks County Courier Times.

*The newspaper, of course! One of the reporters may know what happened.*

I would have my boss check with the newsroom to see if they knew what had happened. Then I remembered it was Saturday. My boss would not be in the building. I went back into the waiting room, sat down, and closed my eyes. I wanted to go to sleep and wake up from this horrendous nightmare.

## /////

The night before, I thought, seemed like ages ago. I had been out with my daughters, Joan and Heather. Joan had been going through a separation, and Heather was just so busy with her special needs baby, Kyle. I had just broken up with my boyfriend and was feeling bummed. The girls and I never seemed to spend any time together unless it was with babies, so we had decided to go out, just the three of us.

As soon as we walked into Michael s Café, the local singles dancing and drinking establishment, off to the left and sitting at a table was a psychic.

*Let's do it,* we decided.

So before we even ordered our first drink, we were sitting at a square table with a large bald man. I cannot remember his name.

Heather went first. For her, it was all good news. She would stay with her husband, Matt, forever. Kyle, her baby who was born with special needs, would progress and do well.

Joan went next. That is when it got very strange. He held her hand tightly. He looked her in the eye and said to her, "If something happens, I want you to promise me you will crawl under the car. Just remember that. Remember to crawl underneath of the car, and you will be safe."

We were firing questions at him that he did not answer. He was making me really nervous and a little mad.

"I'm sorry," he said. "I just feel violence all around her. I can't really explain, but she will be okay." He then asked Joan who Steve was.

"I do not know anyone named Steve," she answered.

He shook his head no.

"Well, my mother's friend Tina has a son named Stephen. He is young, just a little boy."

"No," the man said, "not that one; this one is someone you were interested in romantically."

We all laughed nervously. Steve was a guy Joan had been interested in when she was a teenager. He was the brother of Wally, who was the original drummer in Dave's band.

"I have not seen him in ages," Joan said.

"You will bump into this Steve this weekend," he said.

We really got a laugh out of that. It would be interesting, to say the least, if she did run into Steve. I thought about the time I got a seven-hundred-dollar phone bill, and the girls told me it was Steve. They were fourteen, and he was calling the triple-x numbers. Thank goodness the phone company felt bad for me and removed the charges. I wondered if I should tell his mother. I chose to tell him it had better not happen again. I remembered another time when the girls, Steve, and a few more friends were sitting on the sectional in my front room. A cop knocked on the door. Andy Aninsman said he got a call that a bunch of teenagers were drinking alcohol. They were drinking Slurpees. This town could be like that; the neighbors were so nosy.

Moving on, it was my turn with the creepy psychic. I wanted to know if I would get back together with my ex-boyfriend.

"Not this weekend," he answered.

"Will I ever get back together with him?"

"If you do," he said, "it will not be right; he is not the one for you."

"When will I meet the right one for me?" I asked.

"Not this weekend," he sort of whispered. "Not for a while."

We left that psychic with very strange feelings in our stomachs. We found a table and ordered some appetizers and drinks.

The music was loud. The people were loud. I wondered why I had decided to bring these young girls to this middle-age meat market. We did not stay long. That crazy psychic made us uncomfortable. We decided to call it a night. Heather and Joan did not even want to stop at the diner. That made me a little sad. Heather went home to Matt and Kyle, and Joan went home with me. After what that psychic said, I was glad she would be home with me. We were quiet during the ride from Bensalem to Fairless Hills. It was then that it dawned on me.

*I knew that guy, that psychic.* He had come to my house in Bristol, like, fourteen years before, to do a party. As I thought back, most of what he said had come to pass.

/////

*I will make a cup of tea and watch some television,* I thought, as I turned onto Valmore Road. It was a habit I started a long time ago. I could not fall asleep without the television turned on. I did not feel tired at all. I was thinking about that creepy guy and about how I just wanted to be alone for a while. I didn't even want my ex-boyfriend back. I saw Birna backing out of her driveway.

# SEVENTY-TWO HOURS

I would fall asleep in the waiting room for just minutes at a time. It seemed every time I closed my eyes, a nurse would come in with bad news. The pressure on his brain was rising. I started to think David was not going to make it. I think my mind was preparing me for the worst. I was angry with myself for even thinking it was possible he would not make it, so I prayed. I bargained with God.

*If you let David survive this, I will quit smoking. I will do more charity work. I will go to church more often. Just please let David be okay.* Then I apologized to God for trying to bargain with him. I asked him to make David well.

By this time, newspaper and television reporters started showing up at the hospital. It was the reporters who finally started to give us bits and pieces of answers, and by this time we desperately needed to know how this could have happened. The hospital social worker took us to a room. It was a large room on the first floor where the reporters could ask us questions. We were asking them questions too. The room was next to the gift shop; I could not help but look at all the cute baby stuff in the window. I wished I was there because someone had had a baby.

The reporters wanted to know who David was. What kind of a man was he? It was strange, but they really did seem to care. It was overwhelming, but they were all so nice. I had always heard that reporters were unfeeling, but for us, this was not the case. A couple of them did ask stupid questions, like whether we believed in the death penalty. Who would care about something like that? Overall, they were kind. At the end of that press conference, when most of the reporters had left, Pat Ciarrocchi, a channel three reporter, was still there. She was talking to Birna. Dave and Birna's thirteen-month-old son, Michael, was toddling around. He had not started to walk yet, but he was trying. Ms. Ciarrocchi asked her camera man to film. I don't know why, but I thought that was nice. She had kind eyes. I watched her on the news all the time, and there she was. A real person, there she was, sitting in this huge room in this hospital talking to Birna, and David was upstairs, fighting for his life. I thought about watching the news and the people that are interviewed during tragedies. They always look horrible, and I would think, *Why don't they at least comb their hair or put on some make-up?* Now there I was: I had sat up all night. I had been crying. I looked awful. I just sighed. I did not care. These news people knew more about what had happened than we did, so we needed them. We needed to rely on them for information.

We went back up the elevator and down the long hallway and into the room—the big, empty waiting room. We resumed taking turns sitting with David. Anthony finally showed up at the hospital. His face was red—very red—and his eye was swollen to the size of a tennis ball.

*He should be in the hospital,* I thought.

He told us he had been at the police station in Bristol all night answering questions. He said they had been at band practice. They were rehearsing for the show at the Trocadera, in Philadelphia. The practice went well, and they were all excited about the show. David was driving Joe and Anthony home. A car had been following them closely for some time. They thought it was someone they knew, so David pulled over. When David rolled his window down, the driver from the other car cocked his fist and punched David. Before they realized what was happening, the three of them were out of the car, and they were fighting. David, Anthony, Joey, and three guys from the other car were in the middle of Wilson Avenue fighting. David, Joey, and Anthony were grown men; the other guys were teenagers. The fight did not last long. When the fight was over, Dave offered the kids tickets to the Trocadera show. That sounded like Dave. He never liked any kind of confrontation. They got back into the car. The three of them were stunned and sat there for a few minutes. They decided to just put it behind them and focus on the show. Dave pulled away, still shaking his head.

They did not get very far. They were being surrounded by young men who were beating on the car with baseball bats and hammers. They were screaming for Dave, Anthony, and Joey to get out of the car. Glass was shattering. The three of them decided the best plan would be to run. They did not want to fight again. Enough was enough. Dave popped the trunk to keep them from smashing the back window. Anthony and Joey jumped out of the car and started to run. Several from the crazed gang immediately began chasing them. Anthony ran up onto a porch and began pounding on the door. He was being pummeled in the face with a hammer. Joey made it onto a lawn and was fighting off several attackers.

/////

Mrs. Mulkiewicz was home alone at her house on Wilson Avenue. Her husband worked nights. She heard screaming, glass breaking, and what she thought were gunshots. She peered out of the window of her second-floor bedroom, trying to stay hidden behind the curtain. She was on the phone with a 911 dispatcher, screaming for them to hurry. The dispatcher was asking her to describe what she saw. She said, "There is a man lying in my driveway, and a man in a red sweatshirt is hitting him with a hammer." She described another man in a black sweatshirt stomping on the man's head and another man hitting him with a long object that she could not make out.

As sirens approached, the gang scattered into the darkness like cockroaches. Officers approached Anthony and Joey as they frantically yelled for Dave. The police officers got a call that there was a man down in a driveway on Wilson Avenue. Anthony and Joey ran to him. David was lying in a pool of blood, mumbling "Michael." The first ambulance arrived, but they could not transport him. They waited for another, one with advanced-life-support paramedics. They put Dave into the ambulance and drove off, and Joey and Anthony were taken to the police station.

## /////

That was all Anthony knew. There we all were, waiting in the waiting room. I walked back to Dave's room with Joan. He looked so bad. I held his hand very carefully; it was broken. I was so upset these doctors were not doing anything about the broken bones. I could see them sticking out. I was trying hard to be quiet. They told us not to talk to him; his brain needed to rest so it could heal. I couldn't stop my sobs.

Joan and I walked down the long hall, both of us sobbing with our heads down. We heard someone talking, so we looked up. It was Steve! We could not even speak to him; we just put our heads back down and walked quickly and quietly back into the waiting room. That psychic knew this was going to happen. It wasn't Joan that needed to crawl under the car; it was David. I felt like I was going out of my mind. I was so angry. Did Steve have something to do with this? I had to push these thoughts out of my mind. It was too weird.

I decided to walk out front to have a cigarette. There was a small garden in the front of the hospital. I sat down on a bench. I saw news vans pulling up out front and reporters going into the hospital. It was obvious there was some kind of news, but I did not want to move. I just sat there. I heard a scream that went through my whole body. It was one of those blood-curdling, horror-film screams. I panicked. I knew the voice. It was my daughter Joan. I ran back up to the waiting room as fast as I could. Joan was kneeling on the floor, sobbing. Everyone was standing around her.

She looked at me and said, "It was Jimmy Galione. He is the one that did this to Uncle Dave." She screamed and screamed and screamed. I fell to my knees. My son's childhood friend, he was a neighbor when we lived Bristol. I was so confused. Why would he hurt David?

"Who told you it was Jimmy Galione?" I asked Joan.

"The detective, Randy, said Galione was arrested for assault," she screamed. My son would be coming home. How would he handle this? His uncle was lying in intensive care, fighting for his life. I looked over at my girls; they looked so terrified. I looked over at David's wife, Birna; she was screaming. She looked exhausted. Every time she fell asleep, the nurses would wake her with bad news. I sat down. I couldn't move. I wanted to go to sleep. I drifted off, dreaming of David when he was a baby. I dreamed of waiting at the bottom of the slide for him, so scared because he was so little, and the beautiful smile and giggles when he slid safely into my arms. I wanted him to slide safely into my arms right now!

When I opened my eyes, it was starting to get dark. I scanned the room. The doctor was talking to Birna, saying if David survived, he would never be the same. Did that mean he would be in a wheelchair? Would he have brain damage? If they told us, we were not listening. I just heard "if he survives." That meant there was a chance. A chance was good. David had survived so much in his life: a house fire, falling out of a second-story window, skateboarding accidents, a nail gun shooting a nail into his knee while working on a roof. He survived all of these disasters, and now there was a chance he would survive this one.

I was hungry so I found a phone book and ordered food—lots of food. The waiting room was filling up with friends and relatives. Small groups were chatting quietly. I felt slightly relieved. My son would be arriving tomorrow. I was hopeful he would be arriving to good news.

I spent the evening tidying up the waiting room, talking on the phone, and sitting with David. I would sit in a chair and doze on and off. At one point, I woke and saw a man and a woman I did not know sitting across from me. Their son had been in an accident. A nurse came in to talk to them, and they started to cry. I felt bad for them, and at the same time, I was upset. They were invading *our* space; this was *our* room. I went into the bathroom and did my best to wash up. I brushed my hair and put on some makeup. The sun was coming up. Back in the waiting room, plans were being made to pick up my son and Birna's sister from the airport. I did not want to go. It was Sunday, April 26. The show at the Trocadera was supposed to be that day.

I went back into Dave's room. There was a doctor in the room checking the respirator. I asked him if he was going to remove it, thinking maybe they would see if Dave would be able to breathe on his own. That doctor looked at me like I was an alien. I did not see anything wrong with the question. He ended up just mumbling that they would not be removing the respirator.

The nurses at Frankford Hospital were all so kind. They worked gently with David and were extremely compassionate with all of us. The doctors, well, I suppose they did their best. I knew they were not thinking Dave was some kind of a drug addict. It was hard to read them because they were not as kind as the nurses were. Strangely enough, I had asked in the emergency room if they had screened him for drugs and alcohol. I knew David did not do drugs, and I knew he wasn't much of a drinker, but for some reason, it seemed important for *them* to know.

Birna's sister Elsa arrived from Iceland. She had a son just three months younger than my nephew, Michael. He was adorable. I was relieved she was here for Birna.

*It is an awful excuse for a visit,* I thought to myself, but Birna needed support, and I could not give it to her. While the happy reunion was going on in the waiting room, I walked back to Dave's room. There was a nurse, a doctor, Randy Morris, the Bristol police detective, and Joe Moors, a Bristol police officer, in David's room. They were whispering, but I overheard. David was brain-dead. He would not recover. I was numb. I sat with him for a long time. I walked down the hall, into the waiting room and said nothing. I just sat there. My mother was sitting in a chair, praying for a miracle. My son arrived, and he was talking with his girlfriend and his sisters, still trying to put the pieces together. He was smiling. He was just happy to be home. He had no idea how serious this was. Michael was crawling around on the floor. Birna had finally fallen asleep. I just sat there and cried. I was in a room full of family and friends, and I had never felt so alone.

So many of David's friends and our family members showed up at the hospital to offer us their support and to let us know they were praying. David's friends, Tom Tyrell and his brother, were discussing having him transferred to Thomas Jefferson Hospital or The Hospital of the University of Pennsylvania. My mind started to play tricks on me. Perhaps there could be a miracle. I watched as they hustled back and forth, making phone calls, talking to the doctors, trying to arrange the transfer. The doctors said no. There would be no miracle here.

The benefit concert was supposed to be that day, but all we heard was the rumbling of the respirator and the faint beeping of the monitors. David and the rest of the band had been looking forward to that show. I wanted to be angry; I tried to be angry, but I felt nothing. I just cried, slept, went out to smoke, and cried some more. I felt as if my body was being lifted up and I was floating around by the ceiling just looking down on everyone. People were praying, crying, talking, and sleeping. My brother Nicky was getting angry. It was just his way. I was the oldest, and I needed to pull myself together here and now. It was easy to think, but I could not seem to make that happen.

I thought about when Nick and Dave were little and how much I loved them. I remembered Christmases when they were small and spoiling them with all the best toys. I remembered giving Dave a Stretch Armstrong guy when he was three years old. One morning, he walked up to me with Stretch and wanted to know what was inside. I was busy with Joan, who was a baby, but I started to feel guilty, so I grabbed Stretch and squeezed him. I could not figure out what was inside, so to Dave's delight, I grabbed a knife, and we operated on Stretch. It is crazy, but for the life of me, I cannot remember what was inside that stupid doll. What I do remember was the two of us laughing so loud and me hugging him. Then we went out and bought a new Stretch Armstrong. I can still see him looking up at me and saying, "You are way cool." I remembered the wonderful summer I spent with the boys in Rhode Island.

## /////

The doctors finally told us David was, in fact, brain-dead. He would never wake up. They were just keeping him alive at this point because he was an organ donor. They asked Birna if she wanted him taken off the machines. She was not ready to make that decision. What an unnatural feeling that was—the thought of just *pulling the plug* out of the socket. None of us were ready to play God.

I thought of a time a few years before when my cousin Robin was in a coma. His kidneys had failed. The doctors had asked his wife, Tracy, if she wanted the machines turned off. Tracy, at the time, was nine months pregnant. She decided to wait until after the baby was born. She did not turn off the machines, and Rob recovered.

On April 28, I left the hospital. I had to get out of there. I felt so dirty; I needed to have clean clothes so I went home.

I went into the empty house. I took a long, hot shower, crying the whole time. I sat on my bed wrapped in a towel. I may have dozed off for a few minutes. I suddenly had a strong urge to get out of that house. The overwhelming memories kept me from catching my breath. I felt like I was choking.

I decided to stop by the newspaper building just to let them know what was happening with David and to do a little work. I felt guilty. I was like that when it came to my work and my family. My boss was doing my job. As always, there was a newspaper on my desk. There was an article about the fight. Allen Rubenstein, the Bucks County district attorney, was quoted in the article: "What did Mr. Albert expect when he stopped his car? Tea and crumpets?"

I could not catch my breath, and my heart was racing. I panicked again. This man had *no* idea what happened *that night.* I wanted to drive to Doylestown and punch him right in his face. He was accusing David of starting the fight. My phone rang, and the sound startled me. It was Jill telling me to get back to the hospital. As I was driving back, I was thinking about the ride to the hospital a few nights before. It seemed like a lifetime ago. Was it really just four nights ago?

I walked down that long hallway and saw Nicky sitting on the floor outside David's room. As I got closer, I saw his face in his hands. He was sobbing, and I knew. I wanted to take him into my arms and tell him it would be okay, but that would be a lie. Life would never, ever be okay again. The machines were no longer working to keep Dave's heart beating. He was really gone. They were preparing to take him to another hospital where they could harvest what they could for donation. My sister, Dee, and her husband, Tony, were going with David. Someone had to be there to identify him. What a cruel thing to ask someone to do. I did not want him to leave. I just wanted to go back into the waiting room and wait. I wanted to pray some more for a miracle. I sat there. I was in no way ready to say good-bye. It was all too final. I sat there thinking about my life and about David's life. I wanted to close my eyes and still be a complete family. The rest of that day was such a blur. I thought about my poor sister and her husband, Tony, "identifying" the body. I thought maybe I should try to pull myself together and be strong for my family. I kept having that thought but that was not happening. Most definitely, it was not going to happen that day.

# BRISTOL BOROUGH

Bristol is a small borough in Bucks County, Pennsylvania. Located about twenty-three miles northeast of Philadelphia, along the Delaware River, it is just opposite of Burlington, New Jersey. It is one of the oldest boroughs in Pennsylvania, first incorporated in 1720. With approximately 10,000 residents, Bristol is a small town.

The song "Bristol Stomp" was written in 1961 by Kal Mann and Dave Appell, two executives with the Cameo/Parkway music label, for the Dovells, an acappella singing group from Philadelphia, Pennsylvania, who recorded the song later that year. The song was written about teenagers in 1961 who were dancing a new step called "the stomp" at dances held in a fire hall in Bristol.

As far back as the 1950s and probably even earlier, some young men in Bristol referred to themselves as "Bristol boyz." They likened themselves to the Hollywood gangs of the time.

Also in Bristol were heroin addicts, crack heads, Vietnam-era Veterans with post-traumatic stress disorder, and the Breed, a notorious motorcycle gang.

I grew up in Fairless Hills, another small town, maybe ten minutes from Bristol. As a teenager, I was wary of Bristol. The town had a bad reputation. I heard many stories of drugs and violence. I may have passed through the town twice while growing up.

While house hunting years later, my realtor told me she was taking me to see a house in Bristol. I told her there was no way I was interested, but she convinced me to look at the house. I spent three hours that day at that house. I met all of the neighbors, and my kids were playing in the yard. The house was very old and full of old stuff. There were ten coats of wallpaper on every wall and ceiling. It smelled musty. It was larger on the inside than it appeared. It seemed like a nice family neighborhood, and although I was a little apprehensive, we bought the house.

Living in Bristol that first week, I counted sixteen churches. That was comforting. How bad could a town be if everyone went to church? Of course, I counted at least as many bars, if not more. It seemed like there was a bar on every corner. Warren Snyder, the elementary school in town, was small. It also seemed old, a bit run down. The faculty was warm and friendly and welcomed my kids. My poor Joan had a terrible teacher in her previous school, and I was praying that she would have the kindest teacher this new school had. The principle, John Girotti, was so kind. He said he had the perfect teacher for Joan. My prayer was answered.

Once the kids became involved in the school and sports, it did not take long to feel like we belonged. We finally had a home.

We were busy cleaning, scraping wallpaper, and painting. The first night we stayed in the house, a friend was visiting and decided to play his saxophone. My kids loved hearing him play, and it was relaxing as we scraped and scraped. A man knocked on the door. His name was Joe, and he lived next door. He asked us to be quiet because they had just put their baby to sleep. I was so embarrassed.

We had just moved out of an apartment with three kids, and in a house, we still had to be quiet. A few days later, his wife, Tina, knocked on the door. She was holding an adorable baby boy. She said she could smell bug spray in her house. Apparently, our house had a termite problem that was taken care of before we moved in. We could not smell the insecticide (perhaps because of all the painting we were doing) in our house. I had no idea what to do. I liked them, and I was worried about their baby and my own kids. I hoped we could be good neighbors. I was determined we would get along.

We did get along and spent a lot of time sitting on our front porches. Tina is still one of my oldest and dearest friends.

Down the street on the same side was the Galione family. They had a son, Jimmy, who was the same age as my son, Jimmy, and a daughter, Michelle, the same age as my Jillian. They became the best of friends. They also had a girl, Angela, who was Joan's age, but they never became friends. I got a job working for *The Bristol Pilot,* a small newspaper that was part of a larger group of papers. I started by covering local school board meetings, town council meetings, and such. That was where I got my introduction to politics. What an education. Small-town politics could be complicated, to say the least. Soon after, I became a features writer. I was fascinated by the history of Bristol. There were the Daughters of the American Revolution, the first Pennsylvania bank, ties to the Underground Railroad, textiles, a tea factory (my favorite drink), the historical society and, of course, the song "Bristol Stomp" was written in a house on Pond Street, which was just down the street from our house on Franklin Street.

I fell in love with my new home town and felt very safe. There was always something to do. I would take the kids to the wharf at the Delaware River where we would sit on rocks and eat ice cream. In Lion's Park there were concerts every Sunday evening during the summer. Mill Street was lined with store fronts. Anything you needed or wanted was within walking distance.

I have always loved babies. At twelve, when I found out I was going to have a baby brother or sister, I was thrilled. I was not thrilled that my parents had divorced and this new baby's father was my mother's boyfriend. I did my best to just think about the baby. On September 26, 1970, my little brother Nicholas Charles Albert was born. Two years later, on July 3, 1972, my little brother David Michael Albert was born.

When David was a year old, we had a fire in our house. Nicky, who was three years old, had been in my room and was asking me for cereal. I was tired, so I told him to ask Mommy. The next time I woke up, the house was on fire. Nicky had been playing with matches and set his bed on fire. David was in the crib. I had been sound asleep in the room right next door. I stood in the nursery doorway and saw the twin-size bed with a burnt figure. I thought it was Nicky. David was standing in the crib, crying. I was frozen. My sister pushed me out of the way and grabbed David. When we got out front, Nicky was there on the lawn. That was the first time in my life I remember looking up at the sky and saying, "Thank you, God."

My shock quickly wore off as I realized I was wearing pink footie pajamas, had huge rollers in my hair, and fire trucks were pulling up. I was mortified.

We moved into a rental house close by as our house was being rebuilt. I was sad about losing all my books; I loved to read. I really did not care about losing anything else. Actually, I did not have much of anything else.

While I was sitting at the kitchen table in the rental house doing homework one night, my mother starting praying and asking God to take the evil out of me. You see, the fire happened on New Year's Eve, and a few days before, I'd said to my mother, "You need to water the Christmas tree or the house is going to burn down." For that, I was evil. I took the remark a lot of ways. I was evil because I caused her boyfriend to molest me, I was evil because I did not like her new church, and I was evil because I thought she was the worst mother that ever lived.

A few months later, still in the rental house, I was taking a nap. David was napping in the crib across the hall. The crib was in front of a window, and somehow, David fell out of the window. He fell into a pile of leaves on the patio below. He appeared to be fine. He was just sitting there babbling. He spent a few days in the hospital for observation and came home. How is it possible a nineteen-month-old baby falls out of a second story window and is fine? That was the second time in my life I looked up at the sky and thanked God. It was also on that very day that I first believed in angels and just knew David had one.

A lot changed that year. At sixteen, I got married. While my husband was away in navy boot camp, I spent my days at home with the boys. I knew I was going to be moving away and would miss them terribly. I felt guilty about leaving my brother Frank and my sister, Dede, also. I knew I had to get out of there.

One beautiful fall day, I took David to Washington's Crossing State Park. For hours, I played with him in piles of leaves. I took pictures and could not get over how cute he was. His hair was so blonde, and he had the biggest, icy-blue eyes. He was laughing and so happy. I will never forget that day, and I am so glad I took those pictures. Later that same day, I found out I was going to be a mom. I was only sixteen, but I was ready. I was going to be the best mother. My husband would be home for Christmas, and shortly after, we would be leaving for Chicago. I was so excited and petrified at the same time. I had traveled with my father often; he worked for Eastern Airlines. Moving to Chicago with just my husband and me was different. I knew one thing for sure: not only would I miss my brothers and my sister, I was worried about the environment I was leaving them in and was concerned for their safety.

## /////

Ever since David was nineteen months old, I had a feeling I needed to hold him a little tighter. I knew he would not always be with us. I shared this horrible premonition with David's father (partly because I wanted him to be nice to David when I left for Chicago and partly because I hated him and wanted to hurt him). I thought if I said it out loud, the feeling would go away. It never did.

We drove through a horrible snow storm in Ohio. Road trips were new to me. I had traveled a lot by plane. I felt like such a grown-up.

We moved into the second floor of a house in Zion, just north of Chicago. It had one tiny bedroom, bathroom, and a living/kitchen/dining combination. To the left of us, there were a few houses, to the right, a small patch of woods, and then the Zion nuclear power plant. In front of us was the lake. It was so big. It looked like the ocean, just browner, and the beach was all rocks. The rocks were full of dead fish. I realized it had to have something to do with that power plant. The owners of the house said it was because the power plant released so much hot water into the lake. We had a television, but it never really worked in that house. I was isolated there. While my husband was in school all day, I spent time with the ten-year-old girl who lived downstairs. We would walk through the woods and down by the lake. When my husband was off, we would take long drives through Wisconsin. During the spring, it seemed every night there was the threat of a tornado. I actually saw one once and hope to never see one again. I wrote letters to the few friends I had back home, and the owners of the house let us use their phone once a week to call home. In June, my father brought my brother Frankie to visit and my sister, Dee, who was going to stay with me to help with the baby.

On June 22, 1975, Joan Diane was born. She was the most beautiful baby I had ever seen. I was so comfortable being a mommy. When I think back now, wow—I was seventeen and knew exactly how to take care of her. I did have a lot of practice with the boys and all the babysitting I had done.

I could not wait to get back home and show off my daughter. I was so proud to be her mom. I wondered how Nicky and David would react to the baby. I wondered if they would *even* remember me.

They were curious with the baby. They seemed standoffish with me, and I got the feeling they were mad at me for leaving them. I felt so guilty, because I knew we would be leaving again. I was still in such a dream state with being a mom that it took a while to sink in that things were bad at home. I did not know what to do, so I pretended everything was fine. It was a habit I'd picked up a few years earlier. I was an escapist; it was how I coped with feelings I had no idea how to cope with.

We moved to Newport, Rhode Island. My mother was separating from Nicky and David's father, *finally*, and it was ugly.

I decided to take Nicky and David with me until things were better for them at home. No sooner had I arrived back in Newport with them and David got sick. He had a high fever and ear infections. I found a doctor and got medication for him. I was up the entire night holding him. The next morning, he was covered in red spots. I took him back to the doctor and was told it was chicken pox. Within three days, Nicky and Joanie had them too. She was only ten months old, and it was killing me to see her so sick. I was exhausted and extremely happy at the same time. I knew they were all being taken care of properly.

Once the chicken pox were finally put behind us, we spent the rest of the summer playing at the beach and the playground. I never wanted to give them back, but I knew the day would come. I just didn't think about that day.

My sister ended up moving in with us and met her future husband. Over the next few years, I spent as much time as possible at home. It was a five-hour drive on I- 95. I really enjoyed little league with the boys. Nicky was a terrific player. For him, it came naturally. For David, it was different. He practiced a lot. It was amazing to me how such a small child could work so hard to be good at something. He had so much heart. He did not talk much; he was definitely a quiet one, but I got that because I was quiet too.

Back in Rhode Island, on June 25, 1978, my son, James William, was born. I was twenty years old and had two kids. I had my own *real* family. I had lost a baby a year before Jimmy was born, so it was such a relief to hold him in my arms.

He was gorgeous, and I never wanted to put him down. Joanie loved him too, except for when he was old enough to pull her hair. It was so cute though; she would take his hand and say, "No, no, do not pull sissy's hair." She was only three, but I knew some day she would be a great mom.

My husband would be getting out of the navy soon, and we would be moving home. I found out I was pregnant again. I was a bit shocked. I did want more children, but I really was not getting along with my husband, and the future was so uncertain. We were planning to stay at my mother's until my husband found a job and we could find a home of our own. I decided to have an abortion. This was not me, but at the time, it seemed the best decision. I was sick to my stomach. I had morning sickness with the other two, but this was non-stop sick.

The nurse at the hospital told me it would be at least a two-hour wait. I was so aggravated. Why would they tell you to be there at six in the morning and then make you wait for two hours? I curled up on a chair in the waiting room and fell asleep. I dreamed of the baby daughter I had lost in Rhode Island before I had my son. I was devastated and broken hearted for a long time after that loss. I still think of her every day. While curled up on that chair, I had such a vivid dream of Mary, the blessed mother. She was handing me the most beautiful, tiny baby girl. She said to me, with the most beautiful voice I had ever heard, "She will be a blessing." The nurse woke me and said they were ready for me. Barely awake, I shook my head no, went into the bathroom, got sick, and then splashed cold water on my face. I was shaken. I could not get out of there fast enough. I cried the entire day. I could not believe I'd almost killed my baby.

On June 22, 1980, my daughter, Jillian Denise, was born. She was born on her sister's fifth birthday. She was the smallest of my babies and absolutely beautiful. I just could not seem to put her down. I still thank God and Mary every day for the special blessing I almost did not have.

Nicky and David spent a lot of time in Bristol, and my sister finally married Tony, the guy she had met in Rhode Island, and they bought a house in Bristol too. Nicky played a lot of sports, and David seemed to always be skateboarding. My kids and the neighborhood kids loved to watch him. During this time, I spent a lot of time in the emergency room. David and my son, Jimmy, were both daredevils. In just one week, Dave flipped his skateboard over onto a couple of toes and had to have them stitched. Later that afternoon, my son jumped off the couch and hit the corner of an end table. He had to have stitches in the back of his head. Two days later, David fell off his skateboard and cut his head. Stitches. The day after that, while on a walk down by the river with my sister, my son cut his forehead. Stitches, again. I really thought I was going to be arrested for child abuse that week.

As young teens, Nicky and David spent more time in Bristol. Nicky lived with me for a while, or should I say, he lived with my phone. It seemed he was always talking or fighting with his girl-friend, Belinda.

My marriage broke up, and my ex took my son to live with him in Erie, Pennsylvania. I was heartbroken and really missed my boy. It was the right thing to do, but my heart had a huge, empty hole. As I always did when I could not make things right, I escaped. I thought of everything *except* my son. That is, until I went to bed at night and the house was quiet. It was then that the tears came. I was a failure as a wife and a horrible mother. I prayed to Mary, the blessed mother, and asked her to help me to become a good mother. I asked her to watch over my little boy and to find a way to put me in his heart. I asked her to never, ever let him forget how much I adored him.

One night during a bad storm, I was lying in bed with my daughter, Jill. It was raining hard. We were both scared. We kept hearing noises that sounded like someone was trying to get into the house. I was gripped with a fear I had never felt before. We heard window after window rattle and bang. There were nine windows. I was mentally trying to envision myself locking each one. Could I have forgotten one? Locking windows and doors was a new practice for us. For years, we did not even have a key for our front door. Panic turned to shock as I remembered the window I did not lock was opening. I could not breathe. Jill and I did not talk; we couldn't. We could not even scream. We just laid there listening as the footsteps got closer.

We saw the shadow of a large person. I had a gun, but it was locked in a box in the closet. Why didn't I keep it under the bed? I was trying to come up with a plan to save my daughter, but I was frozen. The shadow appeared in the bedroom doorway, and our screams finally came. It didn't even sound like they were coming from us; the echo was so loud. It took us a few minutes to realize that the shadowy figure was a soaking-wet David. If I'd had the gun within reach, I would have shot my little brother. I cried the entire night, tears of anger and relief. The next day, I was just thankful we were all okay. I could not even be angry with Dave; I just made him promise to yell out the next time he broke in. We all laughed, but I never wanted to feel that helpless and vulnerable again. From that time on, every window was locked, double and triple checked. My premonition of losing Dave was back full force, and I had trouble shaking the visions.

# LEAVING BRISTOL

My mother had gone through yet another divorce and decided she wanted to move closer to her job. I had wanted to take Jimmy and Jill out of Bristol. I decided to buy my mother's house. Joan was living with her boyfriend Dominic, and they were getting ready to have a baby. Jimmy and Jill hated the idea of leaving Bristol, so I spent the next two years driving them back and forth. When I took over the house in Fairless Hills, I inherited my brothers. Nicky was going through a divorce from Belinda, and Frankie, as always, was doing his own thing. David was into his music. He was playing bass with a band called Load, which later switched its name to Plug Ugly.

On September 22, 1995, Allyson Rae Nocito was born. Being a grandmother was amazing. Nothing could have prepared me for the overwhelming feelings I had as I held that tiny girl for the first time. I was brought back to that navy hospital in Chicago where I had held my own daughter for the first time. Allyson looked exactly like her mother. I fell in love with her before she was born, but holding her, I was overcome with love. Where had all that time gone since I held my very own baby girl?

I was not happy with the fact that my twenty-one-year-old daughter was going to have a baby. I tried to talk her into not having the baby, but she was adamant that she was going to have her baby. I could not help but remember my own dilemma all those years ago. I was very proud of Joan for making the right choice. It was all over when I held baby Allyson; I was hopelessly in love.

Nicky did not stay with us for very long. I did my best to create a family atmosphere for the rest of us. Before long, we realized David was falling in love. Birna was adorable, and I liked her instantly. She was from Iceland, and it was fascinating to hear all about a country I had honestly never even thought about. Birna was in the United States working as an au pair. We quickly became friends and spent a lot of time together. I had a foster child at the time, Danielle, and Birna was a great help with her. Au pairs were only allowed to stay in the United States for one year, and then they had to return home for a period of time before they could come back. We tried not to think about that time. When the time came and Birna left us, David was miserable. I was actually worried about his health. He was not eating. I had never seen him so sad. It reminded me of my brother-in-law, Tony, when my sister left Rhode Island, and Tony had walked all over the navy base with a tin cup, trying to come up with enough gas money to go to Pennsylvania and bring her back. He went to pick her up and ended up staying in Pennsylvania.

After a couple of weeks, we sent David off to Iceland to get his girl. She returned, and they were living with us. We were thrilled. The green card process was started and the wedding planned. I was so excited to find out they were expecting a baby. I was also scared, because I thought they would want to move out and get their own place. I was quite relieved to find out that their place happened to be right across the street.

Joan brought Heather home one day from school, and she never left. She had a difficult home life and ended up living with us and became family. I always thought of her as the daughter I lost. She was my long-lost baby girl. I adored her. Heather and her boyfriend, Matt, were expecting a baby.

On September 15, 1997, Kyle Christopher was born. I stopped by the nursery to look at him before going to Heather's room. He was beautiful, but I immediately got the sense something was wrong. I remembered during the summer sitting on my front porch with Heather and rubbing her belly. I knew then something was wrong, but like I always do, I wrote it off to just being nervous. Kyle had a genetic syndrome. I should have been devastated, but I just did not want Heather to lose him. We were all impressed by the way Matt and Heather fought for their baby. Joan was devastated. She felt guilty and did not understand why God gave her such a healthy baby and did *this* to Heather. I did not question why God did this, because I knew the answer. Heather was the perfect mother for this perfect baby. We were told Kyle would not survive twenty-four hours, then two months, and then two years. Thirteen years later, I still believe God gave us this angel and picked out the most perfect parents for him.

David was impressed with the way Heather and Matt cared for Kyle. He also would be a father in a few months. I asked him if he was nervous or scared about the baby being healthy. He said no. He said, "Just like Heather and Matt, I will take whatever God gives."

March 30, 1998, was a beautiful day. The sun was so bright, and it was warm. Birna came over and told me she was having contractions. I told her to relax and go take a shower and get dressed. I told her I would take the kids to school and then we would do some shopping. She said her contractions were getting very uncomfortable, so we headed to the hospital. Driving to the hospital, I looked in the rearview mirror, and I will never forget the excitement in Dave's eyes. As we were walking down the hall to labor and delivery, Birna seemed to be stopping every thirty seconds. I realized what

I thought might be false labor was indeed the real thing. We got her settled into bed, and the nurse told us she was eight centimeters. They could not give her the epidural. To this day, I feel guilty about that. As she was pushing, Dave sat next to her, holding her hand. "Come here," I told him, "your baby is coming."

"No," he said, "you are doing a good job down there. I'll stay here."

I laughed. After a bit of a struggle and help from a doctor and a vacuum, Michael Gisli Albert made his way into the world. What an amazing experience! I felt so blessed to be included in their moment. With Birna holding Michael and David snuggled next to them, I could not believe what a beautiful family they were. There was no doubt in my mind that David would be a terrific father. Michael was a good baby. He was quiet like his daddy and his aunt.

Allyson was two and a half and loved watching her cousin Michael in his swing. I loved watching her kiss Kyle's head. She and Danielle were very protective of both babies.

Dave's band was doing quite well. They were performing every weekend. They also did a lot of underage shows, which thrilled my kids and their friends. I did not care for the kind of alternative music they played, but I was so proud of what a good musician he was. It was neat that the band was becoming quite famous locally. During the week, Dave worked with my son, Jimmy, and my brother Frank. They worked for the Mucci Company as mason contractors. They seemed to have a good time working together and always made us laugh at night with stories of their crazy work day. I looked forward to those evenings on the front porch.

One night, Dave asked Allyson to do a rain dance. I was laughing hard as he danced around the living room, showing her how it was done. After the dance had been mastered, Allyson asked, "Why do you want it to rain?" Dave said he loved rainy days because he could stay home from work, be with Birna and Michael, and play his guitar all day. Rainy days always make me smile now.

Dave and Birna were planning Michael's first birthday. The party was held in the gym at Huntington Valley Christian Academy.

Everyone was there; it was a great family celebration. I invited Blue from *Blue's Clues*. Michael was terrified of the big blue dog at first, but he warmed up to him and gave a few smiles. I can still hear the laughing and see the kids running around that gym. I have a perfect picture in my mind of Dave and Birna standing next to the high chair as Michael took his first bites of cake. It was the perfect memory. We were all happy for a moment.

My boyfriend broke up with me, and I was sad and relieved at the same time. It was just Jill and I in the house. Jill was always in Bristol. I was not used to being alone. It was unsettling at first. I quickly appreciated the time to myself. When I needed company I was thankful to have Birna across the street.

Birna had to continue the green card process. It certainly is not an easy process getting into this country through the front door, but Dave and Birna were determined to do it the correct way. I got such a kick out of watching the two of them preparing their letters and filling out the endless forms provided by immigration. They were both so nervous the day of the interview. I told them they had nothing to worry about; it was very easy to see their marriage was legitimate and they were truly in love.

Two of Dave's friends were killed in a horrible explosion. He was taking it really hard. Dave and the rest of his bandmates decided to do a benefit concert for the families. I was so proud of him. The kids were all excited because it would be an all-ages show, and they would be able to attend. I was even excited about going. It was going to be at the Trocadera in Philadelphia, and that was a big deal for a band.

April 24, 1999, was a warm and sunny spring morning. I sat on the front porch having a cup of tea and soaking up some sun before heading off to work. David came over for his usual cup of coffee. It was so nice out; I did not want to go to work. Spring fever, we decided and then laughed. We talked for a while and then, of course, we both went to work. Later that afternoon, I was sitting on the porch, again with a cup of tea. I was excited to be going out with Joan and Heather later that night. Dave came over for another coffee. He was getting ready to leave for band practice. I told him I was very proud of him for the benefit concert. I also told him I was proud of what an amazing father he was, and I reminded him that he had a terrific wife. I told him I loved him. I'm sure he knew I loved him, and I did tell him often, but on that particular day, I am grateful I told him. As he walked away, I asked if he had my tickets for the show on Sunday. He turned around, smiled, and patted his chest pocket.

"Right here," he said. He smiled again and walked away.

## David's Letter to Immigration

*July 7, 1998*

*I would like to talk a little bit about my wife, Birna. We first met on May 2, 1995, while she was staying here in the states as an au pair. I liked her very much and we became good friends. It took me over two months to get a date with her. She only had four months left of her stay here in this country and she didn't want to get involved with anybody since she had to leave shortly. I finally got her to go out with me and we fell in love right away. We had and still have so much in common. We dated for about a month and then she had to go back to Iceland since her time was up. We still kept in touch by writing letters and talking over the phone. She only stayed in Iceland for two weeks and then came back here to be with me. It was just too hard for us to be apart. Since then she has been going back and forth from here to Iceland. The longest we were apart was three months. That was so hard. I could not live without her. I finally went to Iceland to get her. I was afraid she would not come back here.*

*Now we have been together for three years. Every day I love her more and more. We got married on December 13, 1997. It was one of the happiest days of my life, the other was when our son, Michael Gisli was born. I can't see my future without them, they are my family and I am very proud of them. My family absolutely loves her and they get along great. She is very good friends with my sister and my mother. I'm also very close with her family. I have met her parents twice. We spent five days on vacation with them in Florida and almost two weeks when I went to Iceland. Her brother and sister have been here to visit us. They are all very nice people.*

*I would feel a lot more secure if she had the green card. It scares me to think of us not being together as a family in the USA. As much as I love Iceland, I love my country more and I want my son raised here.*

*David M. Albert*

# ROAD RAGE,
## GANG MENTALITY,
## OR JUST PLAIN
# MURDER?

The definition of *road rage* is: a motorist's uncontrolled anger that is usually provoked by another motorist's irritating act and is expressed in aggressive or violent behavior.

In this incident, this definition seemed to be accurate. David irritated Jerry Reeves by stopping at every stop sign on Wilson Avenue, and there are a lot of them. It was just the way David was. He was a safe and legal driver—always. He did nothing wrong. Jerry definitely exhibited violent behavior, *but* when you make a habit out of cruising around and looking for someone to *fight* or *kill*, does that change the definition?

The definition of *gang mentality* is: a group of individuals who feel invincible and larger in importance, strengthened by the volume of their numbers. The banding together of individuals who may alone be weak and ineffective.

The definition of *murder* is: the unlawful killing of one human by another human.

I think all three happened that night. Bullying also entered my mind. Like me, David had always been easy to bully. David's driving irritated Jerry. Jerry started a fight. When that fight ended, Jerry felt disrespected, so along with his Bristol boyz they attacked David, Joey, and Anthony. That ended in murder.

The news people all showed up at the hospital again. They were all sympathetic and kind. "*Road Rage Victim Dies*" was the headline in all the newspapers and the lead in on all the news shows. Road rage. It sounded to me like a disease, a horrible affliction that can make you kill. It was nothing more than a sorry excuse to slam the claw end of a hammer repeatedly into someone's head, ripping apart flesh and skull bone with every whack. It was obviously a contagious disease, because when one started, the others joined him. I think it was a case of *gang mentality*. One guy was disrespected and had to have his revenge. The others, not wanting to look weak, joined in on the beating. It was not something they discussed; they just acted. Those who were too cowardly to stand for something beat David to death. It was so sad that out of the gang, only two realized what was happening was wrong. My brother was dead.

I honestly do not remember driving home from the hospital. I know Birna was with me. Outside of her front door, there were piles of stuff: diapers, teddy bears, and cards. Birna picked up a small package and read the note. It said, "I do not have much money, but I wanted to do something. I have a son Michael's age, and he always needs these." Inside the package were onesies. Birna and I just cried.

I remember Birna saying she could not understand how people could be so thoughtful and kind and others so evil.

There was a news van parked out front. A nice-looking, well-dressed man approached us. He was from channel seventeen. He asked how David was doing. A lot of things went through my mind, like: *You are supposed to be a reporter, but you are a moron and a loser.* I looked at him and said, "He just passed away." The man apologized and walked away, mumbling that his station was always last. I think I felt sorry for him. Then I realized what I had just said. David passed away. It sounded so smooth and gentle. It just did not sound right. There was nothing gentle about David's death; it was a brutal, horrific, senseless murder.

I walked into the house with Birna. We just stood there. Someone knocked on the door, and the phone rang. I picked up the phone. It was a woman from West Coast Video. She said David had not returned a movie. I said, "He died."

She said, "I know, but somebody has to be responsible for the movie." I hung up on her. I wanted to go to that store and hit her over the head. I wanted to kill her. I just left and walked across the street to my house.

There were people everywhere. There was food everywhere. My father had arrived from Florida. I saw my friend Tina sweeping the floor. I smiled inside.

*God bless her,* I thought.

I walked past everything and everyone and went to my bed. I lay there, just listening to voices, so many people coming and going. I would fall asleep and wake up and still hear people coming and going. If there was talk of a funeral, I did not hear it; I heard nothing but mumbling. I slept and did not dream. It must have been morning, because I smelled coffee and the sun was bright. I went back to sleep. I felt someone playing with my toes.

*Stop that, Dave,* I said.

*Come on. Get up and make me some coffee.*

I jumped up. It had all been a horrible nightmare. I walked downstairs. My kids were all lying around. I felt groggy. There was sorrow thick in the air. I was still in the nightmare. Birna's parents were coming from Iceland, someone told me.

*Good,* I thought, *because I'm not sure I can be there for her right now.*

I made a cup of tea and sat down at the kitchen table. My grandmother was still alive. She was a great-great grandmother. My grandfather had committed suicide a few years earlier. He had been very sick for a long time. It was sad, but I thought of losing my grandparents. I thought of a time when I may lose my own parents. I was *never* prepared to lose a brother. No, there is no preparing for that. Nevertheless, I had thought about losing David. I wish I hadn't. It just wasn't natural. I went back to bed.

I vaguely remember talk of the police looking for evidence. I was just so groggy that I did not care. I remember thinking I should be doing something, but I couldn't do anything. I thought about everything. I thought about when David was born. I tried to imagine what he was thinking as he was being beaten to death. Did he feel pain? They say when you get shot, you do not feel the pain. Did he know he was dying? Was he unconscious as boot blow after hammer blow struck his helpless body? I shook my head hard and tried to make these thoughts go away, but I really wanted to know.

Birna's parents arrived from Iceland. I was so relieved they were there for her. I was having such a hard time trying to pull myself together. I was so sad I wasn't meeting them under happier circumstances. They were such nice people, and I wanted to get to know them. It was just so hard to focus on anything. They told me they loved David and that their hearts were broken. It was very hard for them to comprehend this horrific crime, because murders don't happen in Iceland. In fact, in the year 2000, the murder rate in Iceland was .05 percent. That is a strange number, but that is the way it is listed. Iceland is in the top three safest places to live in the world, maybe the murder rate is so low because it is such a small country or maybe because it is so cold. Whatever the reason, I was sure Birna's parents were worrying about leaving their young daughter and brand-new grandson in the country with the highest murder rate in the world.

Because of David being an organ donor and the necessary autopsy due to the nature of his death, David's body was not turned over to our family for over a week. The decision was made to cremate Dave. I hated the decision. I thought about the house fire and how David could have been burned up then. I could not argue the decision because I just had no strength.

The minister called and asked me about my relationship with David. I told him in David's twenty-six years, I had never had a fight with him. I never even argued with him. I told him I was the oldest; I was very quiet and sensitive. I told him David was the youngest and also very quiet and sensitive. My sister, Dede, and brothers, Frankie and Nicky, were much more outgoing. Dave and I were the calm, non-confrontational ones. We hated discontent of any kind. We were like book ends holding the five of us together. There was going to be a funeral. I wondered who was making all the plans. Did anyone plan anything? I hated that I had to pick out something to wear. There was no way I was going to go out and buy something. The thought of buying something to wear to David's funeral made me sick to my stomach. I decided to wear the dress I had bought to wear to the benefit concert, the one Dave never got to play. It was silver and seemed appropriate to me.

The night before the funeral, my father decided we would all drink. Something I did not do very often. We sat at the kitchen table, talked, and drank. I finished a bottle of Southern Comfort. I did not feel drunk; I felt nothing. I did not want to go to the funeral. I did not want to take a shower, get dressed, and hurry the kids along. I hoped there would be people there. My mind was rambling. I wanted to sleep. People were there, more people than I ever could have imagined. I knew almost everybody. How could I possibly know all these people? I was overwhelmed at how many young people were there. How sad for them to deal with this horror at such young ages. I sat in the front row. There was a coffin, but I knew David wasn't in there.

They burned him. There was a huge photograph of David on a stand next to the coffin. The music was comforting: Cat Stevens's "Father and Son" and Eric Clapton's "Tears in Heaven." I knew these songs were favorites of Dave's. The minister talked about David and all of our relationships with him. Little Michael walked up to the picture of his daddy and just looked up at him. For the first time in weeks, I felt something. I cried, and it hurt. That precious baby no longer had a daddy. The whole church was sobbing. I could not wait for it to be over, and at the same time, I wanted it to last forever. It was final. I had to say good-bye. For the past twenty-six years, I'd had three brothers and one sister. What was I supposed to say now? Was there some kind of rule? Should I still say I have three brothers and one sister? Should I say I had three brothers and one died? Why was I thinking about this now? It seemed urgent. I needed an answer. We stood up in front of that church for what seemed like hours. There were so many people I had not seen in years. Mrs. Bazzolla was there. She was my sister's friend Cherie's mother. I had always liked her. She had lost her husband at a young age and was left with six children. Two of them were still babies. She was a strong woman. She moved from the neighborhood years ago; nevertheless, there she was now to say good-bye to David. One friend that was not there that day was Mark Weaver. He and his family were long-time neighbors of ours in Fairless Hills. He was at the hospital, as his wife was giving birth to a baby boy. They named him David. I was touched deeply.

I was amazed that someone as quiet as David had that many friends. His life had touched *everyone* in that church. I was proud of him. I wished he could see how many people cared for him and were disgusted by what was done to him. Could he see?

There was a book in the hallway for everyone to sign. I saw Randy, the detective, standing next to the book. There were other police officers there. I wondered why. Did they expect one or more of the killers to show up? I felt a jolt of panic. I convinced myself they were just being kind. They asked if they could take the book. I thought that was bizarre, but whatever they needed to do was okay with me.

After the church, there was a lunch at Kings Caterers. David had worked there as a teenager. I remembered one night when Dave had called my ex-husband and said his high school reunion was being held there and that he should come right over. I was quite pregnant with Jillian, so I did not go. My ex-husband was there at the funeral. I was relieved he was there for the kids, because I certainly wasn't. He had always liked David and, after all, had known him since he was a baby. It was so dark in that room. I tried to eat. I saw Michael Piazza. He had been the first baby I ever babysat for. I loved that kid and his sister Michelle. There he was, all grown-up with a wife and a little baby girl.

Over the next few weeks, there were concerts, memorials, and a candlelight vigil. I was once again amazed at the people that turned out to support us. The vigil on Wilson Avenue was heart wrenching. I vaguely remember talking to anyone, but I remember all the faces. The blood was still in the driveway where David was found. I wondered if they were going to clean it up, and the thought made me sad. It should stay there forever. That's all we had left. I wondered if I was crazy because I thought about scraping it up. I just couldn't bear the thought of all that was left of David being washed down a storm drain. How many times had I driven down this road and thought of nothing? How many times had I driven down this road and thought of the night my Jillian was born at the other end of the road? Now what? Would I avoid Wilson Avenue for the rest of my life? That would be hard; my sister lived there. As time went on, I was drawn to that spot. David took his last breath there, and to this day, I feel close to him there.

I remember being down at the Lion's Park. The religious leaders in the town wanted to do something to promote healing. Sixteen churches I counted the first week I lived in Bristol; never in a million years did I ever imagine they would all come together for my baby brother.

I wished it were for some other reason. There was a huge crowd, and up in front of me, I saw Jimmy Galione's mother. My body froze. I turned away and took in the crowd of people that loved David. I appreciated everything everybody was doing for us, but I just wanted to go to sleep.

My son went back to the army. A few days later, he was home again. He just got on a bus and came home. He just wanted to be with us, and I wanted him with me. I wondered if he would be in trouble, but I didn't care. We would deal with that later, not now. Somebody would understand.

There was a scare with Birna's green card. David had been her sponsor. After some frightening conversations with several attorneys and the shock at the cost to keep her here with us, I decided to call Congressman Greenwood's office. I wrote his newsletters. After a few weeks, a rep from his office had everything straightened out, and Birna would be staying. This was such a relief, and I will forever be grateful to them. I was terrified that Birna would have to take Michael back to Iceland.

## /////

The investigation continued. Jimmy Galione was arrested and released on bail. The police finally informed us who was there *that night* and a little about how each of them were involved. The police reported that Jerry Reeves was driving the first car. After the first altercation, the second car pulled up. Mike Good, Steve Owtscharuk, Jim Williams, Mark Cupitt, and Antonio Ruiz were all involved. Mark Cupitt and Antonio Ruiz ran away when they realized the police would be coming. That information was devastating. My kids knew all of these people. I knew most of them. These people had been at a party in Levittown.

My daughter, Jill, was hearing various stories about *that night* in school. When we relayed this information to the police, they investigated. The other people that had been at the party would not cooperate with the police. It was so frustrating. If it was true, I do not understand how anyone could hear someone say they were going to go out and kill someone, find out they actually did, and not be willing to cooperate. I'm sure they were afraid of retaliation. They were also friends. The police cannot make someone testify (so we were told). I also heard the parents of these kids were telling them to shut up and stay out of the mess. As far as I was concerned, they were all cowards. I do not know how they slept at night. I would come forward if someone hurt a duck! And if my kid ever had information like this and could help, I most certainly would stand by their side and urge them to tell the truth.

We learned that the neighbors along Wilson Avenue were terrified to come outside that night. They all thought they heard gunshots. Many of them heard David pleading for his life.

The police chief, Frank Peranteau, assured us the investigation was continuing, and there would be more arrests. He later told us that on the night of the fight, all involved were at the police station. No one gave the same story. No one, that is, except Dave's bandmates, Joe and Anthony. Jimmy Galione wrote a confession. He admitted to hitting Dave with a hammer. Randy Morris, the Bristol Borough detective, wanted to arrest everybody and then sort out the details. I wish he had done that.

There were detectives from the county, attorneys, and the Bristol Borough police combing Wilson Avenue, looking for evidence. They were talking to all the neighbors, trying to sort out who saw and heard what. I did not want to think the police were making mistakes. I had to have faith in them. I prayed they were doing everything right. I have always been a patient person, and I needed to be now more than ever.

There seemed to be something in the paper every day. Sadly, that was where I got most of my information. I had always read the paper every day, long before I worked for the *Bucks County Courier Times*. It was strangely comforting, as if what I was reading was about some other poor soul who had been killed. It was always about someone else *before*.

There was a meeting held with the assistant district attorney assigned to the case. Matt Weintraub seemed like he cared about us. He seemed like he cared about David. I liked him right away and was convinced after listening to him that everyone involved in David's murder would be charged. He had such a nice smile and seemed very confident. The meeting was held on the second floor of the Bristol Borough town hall. The building held the police station, fire station, mayor's office, and the other official town operations like zoning and taxes. I had always liked the building; it was very old. I drove past this building every day for over fifteen years. I had been up on the second floor one time before. My mother married her third husband in the mayor's office.

I tried to understand what Matt was explaining to us. The terms were familiar because I had heard them in movies and on television. But unlike television, it would not be solved in an hour. Randy Morris and the police chief were there also. They seemed to disagree on some points with Matt, but I wasn't really paying attention. I was noticing how my brothers Frank and Nick looked so handsome in their suits. But I could see in their eyes how broken they were. They were trying to be tough. We all were.

## /////

Shortly after that meeting, Jerry Reeves was arrested and charged with homicide. Jimmy Galione was rearrested, and a conspiracy charge was added to his criminal homicide charge. That was such a relief. We had been hearing for weeks that Jerry Reeves had been bragging about how hard he hit Dave. We heard the others were bragging also. Finally, our patience was paying off. I knew it would not be long before the rest were arrested and charged.

# TRYING TO GRIEVE

David's birthday was July 3. My mother wanted to have a birthday party for him. I thought that was weird. We all showed up anyway, and it was really weird. Was I the only one bothered by having a birthday party for a dead person? We celebrate the birthdays of dead people—Presidents' Day, Martin Luther King Day, and of course, let's not forget Jesus.

I remembered learning in psychology class that everybody handles grief differently. There are steps to proper grieving. There is no order in which you follow these steps; you just have to go through all of them: denial and isolation, anger, bargaining, depression, and acceptance. After feeling or going through all of these steps, you can move on, get over it, let it go, whatever. I did not want to handle grief; I wasn't ready. I just wanted to wake up from this nightmare and have David with us.

I started to feel very disconnected from my family—not from my kids but from my mother, sister, and brothers. I wondered why. Had I done something wrong? On the other hand, maybe it was because I was doing nothing. I just slept. I wanted to see a ghost. I wanted Dave to be in my dreams, and I wanted him talking to me just like on that day after the funeral when he tickled my toes and asked me to get up and make coffee. I wanted him to tell me what actually happened and why. I believed in ghosts and angels and thought because I believed, I would see.

Jimmy Galione was released on bail. I hoped I would not run into him. I was so confused. He had been re-arrested and charged with conspiracy as well as the original homicide charge. I thought if you were charged with murder, there was no bail. I had a lot to learn about our justice system. I kept wondering when the others would be charged. Randy, the detective, kept saying to be patient. I had no other choice, so I trusted him.

I woke up one morning and dreaded the thought of getting out of bed. That was my everyday feeling, but on that particular day, I felt so heavy. I realized it was Saturday. Saturday was always the day I slept late. I lay there in my bed for a long time, thinking. I thought about my family. What was going to happen to us? Would we ever be close again?

How in the world would we ever get past this horror? I wanted a cup of tea, so I forced myself to get up. I made it half way down the steps and sat down. I heard voices. The voices were those of my kids. They were talking about me and wondering what they could do for me to help me get through the loss of my brother. I heard Jill saying she could not even imagine losing her brother. I started to cry. I always thought I was a good mother. Really, I was a fake. Oh, I loved them so much it hurt. However, I could have done so much more for them.

Maybe I should have worked things out with their father and stayed with him. I should have sacrificed my happiness for theirs. I had been in relationships that were not always healthy. That was not a good example. My financial situation was like a yo-yo, always up and down. Sometimes I did really well, and at other times, we were downright poor. Everything I ever wanted to be for them, I was not. There I was, sitting on a step, feeling so sorry for myself I could not even function. They were so young to have something this horrific happen in their lives. They still had their grandmother, grandfather, and great-grandmother. This was the first time they had to face death.

I felt guilty. I should have been there for them. I sat on that step and decided that I would pull myself together, and somehow I would be some sort of a role model for these kids. I would find some way to make something good come out of this horror. I had no idea what I would do, but I would figure something out. I went back upstairs and took a shower. I did not cry, but I thought I would just wash all the sorrow off and let it go down the drain. I talked to God.

*This is a very bad thing that happened. I'm not angry with you, God, but I would like to understand.*

My kids were still here. I had Birna and baby Michael. I thanked God for them. I needed to think about my special little babies, Allyson and Kyle.

It never occurred to me to be angry with God or to blame him for what happened to David. I wondered why. Most people are angry with God when tragedy strikes them or even when things do not go their way. I just blamed the murderers and their free will. It was their choice to take David's life, not God's. I have always considered myself a spiritual person. I believe in God and Jesus and consider myself a Christian. I gave up, however, on organized religion. I believe God loves you whether you go into a building to pray or not. I most likely did a disservice to my kids because I allowed my mother to take them to her church. Actually, I really screwed up. Because I was confused about religion, I let the person who confused me take responsibility for my children's religious education. I would most certainly have to find a way to fix it. It would not be this day.

I thought about how I hadn't seen Heather in a long time. Did she need me? My son's girlfriend was pregnant. I should be helping him. Jill just graduated from high school, and she was helping Birna. I got out of the shower and got dressed. I sat on the edge of my bed.

I needed to concentrate more on my job. I needed to work harder. I was not financially prepared for a tragedy of this magnitude, and I was feeling the stress of being out of work for so long.

Going back to work was tough. I had no idea how I would concentrate. Everyone there was so kind to me. I could tell they were nervous, so I assured them that it was okay to talk about what happened. I watched as everyone went about his or her business, and it all seemed so normal. I wondered if I would ever feel normal again. As always, there was a newspaper on my desk. There was an article about the investigation, so I sat there and read. It still was like reading about someone else's life. I do not remember much else about those first days back other than just feeling like I was floating. I was there but not really there.

I was only back to work a few days when I saw the news that Jerry Reeves could not make bail. *Poor, poor Jerry* came from a disadvantaged family and was stuck with a public defender. I took comfort in the fact that he was stuck in that jail. I wished Galione was there too. It seemed like wherever I went, I ran into one of the punks who had been present *that* night. With my job, I was on the road a lot. I had to visit my accounts. I remembered being terrified every time I walked into a WaWa, our local convenience stores. I was not sure at that point if they even knew who I was, but I sure knew who they were.

Whenever I saw one of them, I wanted to scream at them, "Why did you do this?" I wanted to tell them I wished they would rot in hell, but my body always just froze, and then I wanted to just get away. This fear kept me from leaving the house most days. I just went to work, came home, and slept.

Jill moved into an apartment in Bristol with Birna. I was proud of her for wanting to help. My son moved into an apartment with his girlfriend. I really missed all of them. The house was not the same. It seemed like everyone was moving on, and I was stuck. I decided I was going to move also. They say you should not make any major decisions after a tragedy; "they" are absolutely correct. I should have waited. I should not have moved, and I certainly should not have allowed my *boyfriend* to move in with me. Yes, the one that broke up with me right before Dave died, the one who I absolutely knew from my head to my toes was not the right one for me. I did it anyway.

I decided at this point that I had to get some help, so I went to visit my doctor. She suggested I take anti-depressants, but I decided not to. I was already so numb and unable to feel. I decided to give myself a little more time. I was becoming a professional "stuffer." I took all of my feelings, good, bad, and horrific, and stuffed them into neat little compartments in my mind. When my mind became full, I stuffed them in my stomach.

We received the news that Jimmy Galione and Jerry Reeves would be tried together. I had no idea what that meant, but the trial was to start November 16, 1999. I was scared about the trial, yet I was anxious for answers.

It was about this time that NOVA came into my life. The Network of Victim Assistance had actually been there since the day after David died. They were offering to be there for us throughout the trial. They would provide us with court advocates. A court advocate understood the court system, and they would be there to answer our questions. NOVA was also helping Birna with financial assistance from a fund that reimburses expenses caused by a crime. The funeral was one of those expenses. They were nice people, and I made a mental note to learn more about the organization. I was making many mental notes back then.

When I was alone, I remembered what people said to me at the funeral. People really do say some stupid things. My favorite stupid thing was, "He's in a better place." Seriously, whenever I heard this, I wanted to scream, "*What better place?*" The best place for David was here with his wife and son, with his family. Another favorite saying of mine: "Time will help." Who wants to hear that? Nothing will help! *My twenty-six-year-old brother was murdered. It hurt like hell. This is a funeral, and it is awful!* Time helps nothing but the stuffing process.

What I appreciated hearing was, "If you want to talk, I'm here." In addition, I appreciated the people who actually did something, like bringing over food or my wonderful, God-sent friend Tina, who was just there. I just think about her sweeping the floor; it is crazy, but that was so comforting. I also really liked it when people just said, "I do not know what to say." I know everybody is different, and maybe these things would not bother somebody else. I especially appreciated people I did not know sharing stories with me about Dave. I am still blown away by the number of friends Dave had that just loved him.

I started to think about all the people I had known in my life, people I had lost contact with and had not seen in years. I wished I felt like looking them up but not now. I made another mental note to do that someday. I wished I did not feel so alone.

It was about that time, when I was spending so much time alone, that I developed an obsession for shows like *Justice Story, Unsolved Crimes,* and Lifetime true-life movies. I had promised myself I would do something to show my kids that there was a way to rise above tragedy. In all of those Lifetime movies, it seemed there was someone who rose above horrible circumstances and did something great. I would just lie in my bed, watching movie after show; I told myself I just needed time. I started to keep a journal. I did not want to forget my baby brother or any of the feelings I was having.

I was worrying about the trial. I was convincing myself I would feel better when at least some justice was served. I was angry there had still been no other arrest. I really wasn't angry; I wanted to be angry, so I just pretended to be.

I was wondering what it felt like to be Jimmy Galione's mother, to know that the son you had carried in your belly and given life to and had loved and taken such good care of had taken someone's life. It was not just anyone's life, but the life of a good man—a husband, a daddy, a son, brother, and friend, a man who was adored. What would it feel like to know your son took the claw end of a hammer and slammed it into a man's head over and over while he was pleading for him to stop.

I wondered what it would be like if it had been my son. What if I got that phone call saying, "Your son has just been arrested for murder"? My son, Jimmy, grew up with these people. What if he still hung around with them? I really tried to feel sorry for Galione's parents. They did not deserve to have a criminal for a son or brother. They, however, were in denial. That fact made me hate them. If it were me, I would have told my son to be a man and tell the truth. I mentioned these thoughts to my son, and he convinced me there was a difference. He said there was a reason he no longer hung out with them. He also said he just could never hurt anyone like that. I believed him.

I also realized had anything like that ever happened with my son, I would still love him. I would also have compassion for the victim's family. On the other hand, at that point, I did not feel sorry for Jerry Reeves's parents. I knew he had been in trouble before. I heard he had hit his girlfriend's father over the head with a heavy frying pan. That kind of anger does not happen overnight. Why hadn't his parents done anything about his violent behavior? They had to have seen his anger escalating. Maybe it was because I didn't know them. I didn't know Jerry when he was a little boy. I thanked God *my* son was not a murderer. I thanked God my kids were all kind people. I made a mental note to never again complain about anything they ever did. I had to fight all this anger and hatred I felt; I did not want my kids to become consumed with hatred.

I was forced to think about my opinion of the death penalty because people kept asking me how I felt about the subject. I do not think I had an opinion at that time. It was not something I wanted to think about, ever. The owner of the Levittown News World, a little store in Fairless Hills that Dave and I frequented, said if this had happened in his country, they would march the guilty down the middle of the street, and everyone would do unto them what had been done to Dave. What a pleasant thought, if only for a moment.

I tried to imagine myself with a hammer and a bat, just pounding away at *them*. An eye for an eye, it is, in the Bible, right? The truth is, I could not do it. The thought of hurting *anyone* like that made me sick to my stomach. It was just not right. However, was the death penalty right? I concluded in my mind, it was. I also concluded it is *not* right, the way it is in now in America. It is a joke. It takes too long. I believe every legal step should be taken to prove guilt beyond a reasonable doubt. It should just be done faster. I must admit the thought of this whole *gang* sitting on death row was a pleasant one. I waited day after day, wondering if it would be the day. Would that be torturous? I hoped so. David was tortured. I hoped they heard Dave's pleas in their sleep. I hoped every time they closed their eyes, they saw baby Michael's innocent little eyes. I wanted them to feel every pain David had felt.

I wanted to know what David felt. I was obsessed with these thoughts. How do you even imagine lying in a driveway and being hit with the claw end of a hammer and kicked in the head, stomped on by boots, and punched all over your body? I tried to imagine his pain. I tried to imagine what was going through his mind. I couldn't imagine. I still can't. I just prayed that David had lost consciousness quickly and was asleep. I prayed that his guardian angel shielded him from the pain.

I remembered in the hospital the nurse telling me that Dave's kidneys were smashed, his liver was torn, his leg, arm, hand, and fingers were broken, and he had several skull fractures. Dave was a big man. I tried to imagine how hard someone had to hit a man as large as David to break a bone, to break a thick bone, like his. When I would have these thoughts, it was just for a minute or two. I couldn't bear more than that. I would get nauseated, and then I would feel guilty. I wondered if anyone else in my family was being tortured by these thoughts, but I could never get the words out. One thing was certain: I was beginning to feel. It happened in spurts, but I was clearly starting to feel anger and sadness.

I have no idea how I managed to go to work every day. I just did what I had to do. I sold ads for the *Bucks County Courier Times*. I think my customers felt sorry for me, because they seemed to be buying many ads. My boss left the company, and my partner moved to another department. I was my department. I just went out every day and came back to the office with ads. No one bothered me.

Everyone looked at me like they felt sorry for me, and that was awful. I had a few *good* work friends who were not afraid to ask real questions. I believe they genuinely were concerned about my feelings.

It was starting to get cold out, and the date for the trial was quickly approaching. Would I get any answers? Would these other killers ever be arrested? Would I feel any better when this legal stuff was all over? I suddenly panicked, thinking the trial would be starting on November 16, a week before Thanksgiving, and before long, it would be Christmas; how would we ever get through the holidays?

I convinced myself it did not matter. I didn't care about Christmas, not this year. For twenty-six years, I had a baby brother for Christmas. I had great memories of every one of them. I remembered when he was two years old and was wearing a blanket sleeper with the feet cut out. It looked so funny, but he had the biggest smile and was just so cute. Just last year he was here. It had been Michael's first Christmas. Dave and Birna were married on December 13. My heart just broke, thinking of that poor girl. There would be no happy anniversary this year. Twenty-six years of memories is a lot, and I was terrified of forgetting any of them. I pulled out my photo albums and spent hours going over them. I would slide my finger over David's face in the photographs. I closed my eyes and imagined I was burning every image in my mind.

## /////

One week before the trial was due to start, we were told there would be a delay. There would be no trial until January. When I heard that news, I was angry. I actually *finally* felt so angry it scared me. I was convinced the trial was being delayed until after the holidays so Jimmy Galione could spend the holidays with his family. It was the first time I had cried in months. I hated them, the whole Galione family. The thought of that killer having a nice Christmas with his *whole* family just hurt. My body actually burned. I wanted him in prison so my broken family could salvage some kind of a Christmas.

My first experience with the American justice system was not going well. I just did not understand why they had the right to delay the trial. I was really getting angry that, not only was the delay of the trial ruining my Christmas, it was taking away the anticipation of the birth of my new grandchild. I could really think of nothing but wanting Jimmy Galione in prison and the others to finally be arrested. I felt completely robbed of all emotion.

## /////

My kids were all living back in Bristol. I cannot say I was happy about that. Dave was killed in Bristol. The killers all lived in Bristol. The killer's families and friends lived there.

Birna was at the mall one day and had an altercation with Jimmy Galione's girlfriend. Yeah, the girl that washed Galione's bloody clothes *that night*. She started screaming at Birna. Birna had Michael with her. Can you imagine how callous a person has to be to scream at a widow who is with her baby? That scared all of us. I was now worried about the safety of my entire family. I could not figure out why these people were angry with us. It didn't make any sense to me. I just could not convince my family to leave Bristol. My kids said they were not going to let the killers take their town from them. I was proud of the way they felt, but it did nothing to ease my fears. I wish I felt that strongly about my hometown.

It was hard for me to go to Bristol at that time. There was a make-shift memorial for David close to the spot where he was found. It was slightly comforting. I honestly am now affected every time I see any such memorial—crosses on the highway, flowers scattered by the side of the road. I always wondered who they were, who their families were, and how they were doing. I wondered how many other people actually took the time to notice. I once heard a woman say she thought they were eyesores. I bit my tongue. I know the comfort they provide. I also got a sick pleasure out of the fact that the killers and their families had to see the memorial and be reminded every time they drove by. My brother-in-law, Tony, was very diligent with the upkeep of the memorial. He and my sister lived less than a block away. David loved to stop at the Wawa in Bristol for a cup of coffee and cigarettes. It always brought a smile to my face when I stopped by and saw a cup of coffee and a pack of Marlboros by the angel's feet. I hoped people would always remember. I was so afraid people would forget.

I was really getting frustrated waiting for the other seven people to be charged. Months were going by. The police kept telling us to be patient. My patience was running out. They were out there, living their lives, and probably never thought about David or what they had done to his family. I was obsessed with wanting to know every detail of what each of them had done. I did not want to imagine anymore; I just wanted to know.

I realized I had not seen the car. I asked Randy what happened to the car, and he said it was evidence and suggested I not go to see it. I had to go. I was not prepared for what I saw. I wondered how much more my mind could take. I was trembling and could not stop. Every window was broken, there were dents everywhere, and the car seat had been ripped out. The seat belt holding the car seat in place had actually been ripped. *Who* could do that to a baby seat? I heard through the Bristol Borough grapevine that it was Steve Owtscharuk. I did not know much about him. I know I wanted him charged with something. How could they have done this? They knew he was the father of a baby. I am not proud of some of the thoughts I had about him. I saw him in Wawa one day, and it was so hard not to scream at him. I wished that he would have a baby one day and that he would be in a horrible accident with his baby in the car seat that was so mangled he could not rip the seat belt and save his baby. I could not believe I even thought of such a thing—not that I felt guilty about wishing harm on Steve, because I did. I did feel guilty about wishing harm on an imaginary baby. I convinced myself it was part of the grieving process. I was angry!

I could not shake the image of that car. Did they do all that damage while Dave was still in the car? Did they come back and do more damage after they left him in that driveway bleeding to death? Is that why Joe, Anthony, and Dave decided to run from the car? Did they fear for their lives? I would have, had someone been pounding on my car with that much force and anger. I would have been terrified. Dave had been hit with his own level, the one he used for his masonry work. He kept it in the trunk of his car.

Maybe Joe, Anthony, and Dave were going to try to grab the tools and use them to get away. On the other hand, the bad people could have gotten the tools after Joe, Anthony, and Dave ran away from the car.

Dave had glass fragments stuck in his face. I saw them that first night in the hospital. He had to have still been in the car while the windows were being smashed. I imagined when Dave got out of the car, he was immediately hit over the head with something and was injured and confused. Was this why he never caught up to Joey and Anthony? Why was I driving myself crazy trying to figure this out? David was dead; did the horrific details really matter?

I really wanted to know what was going on with the investigation. I was not hearing much. I feared the police were busy preparing for the trial and not preparing to arrest Jimmy Williams, Mike Good, and Steve Owtscharuk. I wondered if the two cars had been searched that night. Where was the other hammer? It could be anywhere. It could be at the house where the party was held that night. I felt it was most likely at the bottom of the Delaware River. I heard that through the Borough grapevine too. It was getting harder and harder to believe the good people always win. David was one of the good people. Without a doubt, he was a good person. I was hanging onto my faith by a thread. Not that I questioned my belief in God, I was just having trouble believing he was going to make all this make sense. I had to believe the bad people would pay. If I lost that thought for a moment, I feared I would lose my mind.

Christmas came and went. It is like a blur, and I do not remember much. I just wanted it not to be Christmas anymore. The New Year was coming, the new millennium; we had all been so excited last year, but I did not want 1999 to end. It just was not fair that Dave wouldn't be there. I thought about how much fun it would have been to talk with him about all the hype. Would we lose power? Would computers all over the world crash as predicted? Would we not be able to use ATMs? That would have been a great conversation. Dave would have laughed it all off. I missed him.

His band would have most likely been playing somewhere exciting, and I would have volunteered to babysit so everyone could go. I would have stayed up and waited for them to come home and tell me how exciting the night was and how great the band sounded. Instead, I stayed home and was sick with a stomach virus.

*What a great year this is going to be,* I thought sarcastically.

I did have a new grandchild expected in January. We did not know if it would be a boy or a girl, but my son was going to be a daddy. He had been such a cute little boy. It was hard to think of my son without thinking of David. They looked so much alike and always had a great time together. My son loved sports, and so did Dave. They both loved the Flyers. It had been one crazy year for my boy. He was only twenty-one and had a lifetime of emotions to deal with. I was worried about him. I felt like a bad mother.

I was not emotionally available to anyone, especially my kids. I was not helping them deal with this tragedy.

*Maybe when the trial is over,* I told myself.

I hoped I could make it up to them then. I hoped they would forgive me.

So much for grieving—I just wanted to sleep. I knew I needed help, but I did not want help. I wanted justice, and I wanted it right away.

I knew the way my whole family was feeling was not healthy for Allyson and Michael. They were fed, dressed, and hugged. This was fine, except we were not emotionally available to them. I knew how important it was for them, and I could not make myself shake the sadness, and that made me even sadder. I prayed for guardian angels for each of us, to watch over us until we were feeling better.

# THE TRIAL STARTS

Prior to the trial, there were pre-trial hearings held. Mike Good and Jimmy Williams were supposed to be witnesses. They wanted immunity in exchange for their testimony. I was so relieved—Matt, the assistant district attorney assigned to prosecute this case, refused them immunity. Then Judge Heckler excused them from testifying. If they were on the witness stand, they could incriminate themselves. Matt, the police chief, and the detective asked us to be patient again. They assured us *everyone* who was responsible for David's death would face murder charges.

I would have found all this trial stuff very exciting if it were not for the fact that it was to convict my baby brother's murderers. This was not exciting. It was frightening. I felt so lost in the big court-room filled with people.

NOVA, Bucks County's victim service agency, sent us two court advocates. They sat with us, held our hands, provided tissues, and answered every question we had. They were wonderful. They made us feel protected.

A jury had to be selected. What a long process. All three attorneys had to question one hundred Bucks County residents. They had to all agree on fourteen. I got my first look at Jimmy Galione's attorney. I disliked him immediately. I guess it was normal to dislike him, but it was more than the fact he was representing Galione. That was his job. I hoped he was a decent attorney. If he made any mistakes, we learned that could cause Jimmy Galione to walk free. Matt, on the other hand looked confident. One by one, possible jurors were asked questions. The attorneys argued back and forth. That process took all day. By late evening, the jury pool narrowed to thirty-nine people. They had to agree on twelve and then two alternates. The judge would occasionally call for breaks. Judge Heckler was the judge assigned to the case. He was a large man and looked imposing. He looked smart and in control. I hoped he would be mean. I also hoped he would be compassionate and fair to Dave. I hoped he would really pay attention and listen to who David was.

I do not remember noticing Jerry Reeves's attorney that first day. Jerry had a public defender. I had heard that Jimmy Galione's parents had to sell everything they had to pay Mel Kardos. I also heard that his mother, who worked at Lower Bucks Hospital, was trying to start some kind of a fund to support her son's legal fees. I heard no one contributed. That thought was comforting. She should have been raising money for baby Michael. That would have been the right thing to do. I would have done something like that if my son were the *murderer.*

I wondered about the jurors who were chosen. Would they take their job seriously? Would they get along with each other? I hoped that they were at least honest and compassionate people. I said a prayer for them and all of their families.

The media was there in full force. They were asking many questions. I was glad they had not forgotten David. Our court advocates and Matt warned us we were going to hear graphic details of David's injuries. I was prepared; I wanted and needed to know every detail of that night.

The district attorney, Allen Rubenstein, left office and became a judge. I still hated him because of his "tea and crumpets" comment. He was replaced by Diane Gibbons. We heard rumors the assistant district attorneys did not care for her. They called her a bully and much worse. I hoped it would not affect us. I hoped at least she would be on the side of justice.

All of the preliminary hearings were finished, and the jury was in place. The trial would be starting the next day. I did not sleep that night. I tried to imagine the details we would hear. Was I really prepared to hear them? A thought popped into my head.

*Jimmy Galione and Jerry Reeves will be in the courtroom tomorrow.*

I felt panicked. I had to have known they would be there. How would I contain my emotions? Would my kids be okay? There really was no way to prepare them. I just kept telling myself to remain calm and focused. We all had to keep ourselves calm.

I remembered learning that your mind only allows you to process bits and pieces of trauma at a time. Here I was, lying in my bed, scared to death about seeing my brother's killers face to face, just imaging what the details we hadn't heard would be. I started to obsess about what I was going to wear. I lay there imagining everything in my closet. Did I want an outfit that would make me look sad and in mourning? Did I want one that made me appear strong and confident? Why did I care?

*I am absolutely crazy,* I told myself. I closed my eyes and prayed for Matt, the jury, my kids, the witnesses, and my family. I prayed for strength.

# FIRST DAY OF TRIAL

It was a cold morning. I had to stop at work before heading to the courthouse. I hated the cold. It would be such a long walk from the parking lot to the courthouse.

Opening statements would happen this morning. I was a nervous wreck. I thought about all of the work I would be missing again.

The courtroom was crowded. My whole family was there. I saw our court advocates right away and felt better. I expected a lot of media, my family, and friends to be there. What I had not expected was the large group of people there to support Galione and Reeves. That really surprised me. I really didn't expect the attitudes they had toward us. The nasty looks and comments hurt. I would have expected some shred of compassion. It was hard enough, and then we had to deal with them.

I noticed right away a life-size photo of Dave at the front of the courtroom. I had not expected that, but it made me feel like he was there.

In his opening statement, Matt Weintraub said he would put witnesses on the stand that would testify that David, Joey, and Anthony were so terrified they tried to flee. They banged on doors begging for help.

"This is a case of senseless violence," Matt said.

It was chilling. I watched the jurors' faces as Matt was speaking. I was glad they seemed to be paying attention. Matt was impressive.

Jerry Reeves's attorney was Peter Hall. He was a public defender. He was somewhat dumpy looking but seemed professional. He seemed annoyed by Matt's opening statement. Mel Kardos, on the other hand, seemed fidgety. He was shrugging his shoulders and rolling his eyes. Perhaps I just did not like him. I know I did not like him. I could not help thinking he should have just told his client to tell the truth, to say, "Yes, I hit him in the head many, many times with the claw end of the hammer. I am very sorry, but I am guilty." I may have felt differently. I may not have.

Jimmy Galione looked ridiculous, like an overgrown Catholic schoolboy. He was dressed in dark blue pants, a dress shirt, and a dark-blue sweater vest. He did not look sorry. He looked like a liar. He occasionally turned around and smiled at one of his family members. I wanted to puke.

Jerry Reeves looked uncomfortable. He kept his head down most of the time, especially when Matt was speaking. At least he looked guilty.

Let me tell you, it takes a lot of self-control to be in this position. I love my country. I do believe in our justice system, but there is a lot that could be improved. Sitting in a courtroom with David's killers was bad enough, but sitting a few feet from those who were there to support these killers—that was just pure torture.

Matt explained to the jury he had the picture of David blown up so they could get a sense of who he had been. David was not there to speak for himself. That was comforting and painful at the same time. Matt also explained the meaning of *conspiracy*. He also talked about *gang mentality:* when a group of young men are together and one does something wrong so the others jump in. They do not want to be left out or made to feel weak. That statement angered me. My son told me he was incapable of inflicting such pain on another human being because he knew it was wrong. Two of the people who were there that night knew it was wrong; they ran away. I wondered if they really felt it was wrong or if they just didn't want to get in trouble.

Matt continued to explain that, at a football game, when the crowd rushes the goal post at the end of the game, nobody really stops to think that it is the wrong thing to do. They just do it because everyone else is doing it. That does not make it right.

So much attention was given to the hammer that killed Dave. He was definitely struck by the one he owned. It took the police a long time to find *that* particular hammer. They never found another one. I know there were baseball bats. Every window in Dave's car was smashed. There was no way this was caused by *one* hammer and a level.

Mel Kardos, at one point, actually tried to accuse my brother-in-law, Tony, of taking the hammer from the scene. I never did figure out the point of that waste of time. It made no sense, and he certainly did not try to make it sound believable.

My nerves were getting the better of me. I wondered if the police had made mistakes. There were not a lot of murders in Bristol. In fact, prior to David's murder, there had only been two. My body became very heavy, and I felt dizzy. *Both* of those other murders were unsolved. Back in the 1950s, a little girl had been found murdered in the loft of Saint Mark's Church. The town was split. Half believed the priest was guilty, and the other half believed it was a transient. A few years back, a man was found dead on Mill Street. He was just dead in the middle of the street. They ruled it a murder, but the killer was never found. I had to convince myself the police in this case knew what they were doing. They know who was involved. This case *would be solved;* I had to believe this.

The hours really seemed to drag on and on. Not that listening to Matt speak was boring—it was anything but boring. It was just physically and mentally draining. He was talking about David's job, the band, and his family. He talked about David's personality. He talked about his relationship with Birna and how much he had loved being a daddy. I tried so hard not to cry, but I could not help myself; the tears came. I saw tears in my daughter's eyes, and I wanted to hug her. The huge, imposing picture of David was getting to me. I wanted to hug David. Just when I thought I could not stand sitting there another moment, the judge called for a lunch break. It was hard to stand up. My body felt so weak. I could not wait to walk outside into the cold. We went across the street to Maxwell's restaurant as a family. We were all quiet. We had been completely overwhelmed with emotion.

When Jimmy Galione's family walked into Maxwell's restaurant, we all froze. Why did they have to come *here?* Why did they glare at us as if they hated us? I was hungry and tried to eat. I managed some soup and a half of a sandwich. None of us were looking forward to spending the afternoon listening to Peter Hall and Mel Kardos. I could not even imagine what they were going to say.

## /////

Mel Kardos was first with the defense's opening arguments. He said Jimmy Galione had nothing to do with the blows that killed David and DNA would clear his client. He said he would prove someone else caused the fatal blows and that the fatal blows were not even caused by a hammer. He said his client was a nice young man who just happened to be in the wrong place at the wrong time. He said David, Joey, and Anthony had started the fight. He said they were grown men and his client was just a young man. I wanted to grab the judge's hammer and smash it over Mel Kardos's head. I tried to convince myself he was just doing his job. He was being paid a lot of money to convince the jury his client was innocent.

I wanted to scream at Galione, "Do you even have a shred of a clue of what you have done?" I hated the smug look on Galione's face as his attorney was claiming his innocence. I closed my eyes and just prayed as Kardos continued to blame everyone else for David's murder. He blamed the police, stating they had botched the case from the beginning. I think the judge could sense when we couldn't take anymore. He called for a break. I ran into the bathroom and vomited.

When I came out of the bathroom, I happened to glance up at a catwalk that ran across the upper floor. I saw a woman standing there wearing a dress and sneakers. I did not know who she was, but she gave me a creepy feeling.

There were strict orders about chewing gum in the courtroom, but I needed some. I hoped no one would notice. I made a mental note to bring mints the next day.

It was time to go back into the courtroom and listen to Peter Hall. Would he tell us what a good little boy his client was? Just looking at him, one could see the rage in his eyes. I did not know his family. I did not want to know them. At least Jerry looked like he was in trouble; he even looked sad. Perhaps he was just upset because he was caught this time and was not going to get away with killing.

Peter Hall admitted his client struck David. He was a short, sort of heavy man, this Peter Hall, and his suit was baggy. He seemed annoyed. Of course, he too blamed everyone else there *that night* for inflicting the fatal blows. He said Jerry acted in self-defense. The police were pressured to make an arrest in this case because of the media coverage and the family's pressure. The police settled on Jerry.

I used to feel sorry for people that had rough childhoods. Now, I believe it is an excuse to make bad choices. Everything you do before you are eighteen is your parents' fault; after that, it is your own fault. If you have an anger problem, get help. Is it hard to realize that driving around looking for someone to beat up is wrong? I had a bad childhood. I actually had a horrible childhood. I am not going to kill anyone. I am not going to blame anyone. Maybe my parents did the best they could; maybe they didn't. It didn't matter;

I just put it behind me and grew up. I wanted to be a good person and a great parent. I wanted my kids to have a better childhood than the one I had.

I was so thankful for Mia and our other court advocates. They validated our feelings. They also seemed to be comforting my kids when I was feeling guilty I was unable to comfort them. My stomach started to hurt again. I wanted to go home and go to sleep.

I wanted to see Allyson. My little granddaughter always made me smile. She helped me feel like I had a reason to go on. I made a mental note to bring her to this area of Bucks County one day and explain the history to her. I wanted her to grow up to appreciate the beautiful surroundings so close to her home. I did not want her to grow up thinking Bristol was the only place on earth. There were so many people in Bristol who felt that way. They just never went anywhere. They grew up hearing "Bristol boyz stick together." I heard that saying many times. It never bothered me until it had a dark and sinister meaning. It was no longer an "I'm proud to be from Bristol" statement. It meant kill someone, do not *ever* speak to the police, and never, *ever* tell the truth. It was sad, very sad, that such a quaint, small river town was now divided. Half of the residents of Bristol supported Galiones and Reeves's, and the other half supported my family.

# SECOND DAY OF TRIAL

I was so exhausted, I actually slept through the entire night. Anxiety hit full force as I dressed and got ready to head to the courthouse. I was running late, so I did not stop at work. Once again, the courtroom was crowded.

Matt called my brother Frank to the stand. Frank was so handsome and strong. He was a grown man, but he would always be my little brother. He looked scared. I just kept looking at him and thinking, *Be brave, Frank*. He answered all of Matt's questions strongly, until Matt asked about the level. Frank and Dave worked together. Frank broke down as he explained he had given that level to Dave. It was a four-foot, metal mason's level. My heart was breaking for him. I wanted to run up and give him a hug. I wanted to bring Dave back for him. My throat hurt so badly. I was forcing myself not to scream, and it hurt. Frank made it through the testimony. I was so proud of him. David would have been so proud. I started to imagine what it would have been like if David had survived. I imagined him sitting in the courtroom in a wheelchair, listening to how much his older brother loved him, being there and able to point a finger at every one of the people who attacked him. I was quickly shaken back to reality.

Matt called Mark Cupitt to the stand. Mark lived two houses to the right of my sister. He had always been a nice kid. My son was friends with him. Mark testified that he had been driving the second car that night. He said he pulled up next to Jerry Reeves's car and saw Jerry smashing the windows of Dave's car. He said Jerry was using a level. He testified the group had scattered after realizing the police had been called. He then said they met at a house they had been at earlier for a party. Everyone was talking at once, Cupitt testified. He said Jimmy Galione was imitating how he had repeatedly swung a hammer at David's head. He said Jimmy Galione had blood all over him and washed his hands. I could not believe what I was hearing. It appeared the myth of the Bristol boyz sticking together was unraveling. I was angry at Mark for being there that night but was so relieved he had the guts to do the right thing and tell the truth.

Mel Kardos and Peter Hall were clearly upset. They kept objecting. I hated that word, *objection*. It was such a waste of time. Mark continued his testimony. He said Jerry Reeves imitated hitting David with the level. He said it was as if he were swinging at a carnival game, trying to ring the bell. I kept telling myself to keep my eyes open. I could not close my eyes and see the vision of David lying on the ground and these animals swinging at him. I wanted to scream. I wanted to run away. More than anything, I wanted to know the truth, so I kept my eyes open and listened.

Galione and Reeves showed no emotion. I looked around the courtroom. My family was stunned. Every one of them had tears in their eyes. The judge had to tell the Galione and Reeves families and friends to be quiet. They were actually threatening Mark. They were glaring at him. It was at that point I realized how brave he was. That could be very dangerous for him. He must have had a good family. He was doing the *right* thing. I felt sorry for his parents, and I was very thankful to them for being strong enough to guide their son to tell the truth. I could only hope more of them would step up and tell the truth.

Rich and Dawn DeLuca lived on the corner of Wilson Avenue and Roosevelt Street. The couple each testified they had been woken around midnight by a commotion in front of their house. Once the police left, the couple testified, they saw approximately seven young men gathered around a car. They were all high-fiving each other. One person was gesturing with his foot. He was lifting it up and stomping it down on the ground. That person was saying very loudly, "Every time he begged me to stop, I stomped him again." They could not identify the person doing the bragging; it was too dark. One by one, other neighbors testified. They heard the fight and called the police. They all testified they were too frightened to go outside because they heard what they thought were gunshots.

David was found lying in a pool of blood in a driveway on Wilson Avenue. The woman who lived in that house, 2313 Wilson Avenue, Loretta Mulkiewicz, was home alone. She testified that she was scared to death. She also testified she was looking out of her window and could hear David begging for his life.

"Don't kill me. I have a kid," she said she heard.

The man in the red sweatshirt just kept hitting him and knocking him back down, she testified.

I could not take it anymore. I didn't even think; I just got up and ran into the hallway. My sister, Dede, was right behind me. Loretta's words were just swirling around and around in my head.

"*He was alive and begging for his life,*" I screamed.

I could not stop crying. Our NOVA advocates joined us in the hallway. They did their best to comfort us. I'd wanted to hear everything, and I was upset with myself for running out. I had to go back into the courtroom. Getting in and out of a courtroom while a trial was in process was daunting. The judge gave me stern looks. Everyone looked at me. I was embarrassed and very angry with myself.

Loretta was still on the stand. Mel Kardos was questioning her. What a strong woman. She knew exactly what she saw, and as hard as he tried to twist it and turn it to get her to change her story, she was telling the truth and never wavered. That poor woman witnessed a man beaten to death in her driveway. She, like us, would never be the same. I wanted to hug her and thank her and tell her it would all be okay. On the other hand, what if she had opened her window and screamed for them to stop? Would they have stopped sooner? I had a right to ask these questions. I knew in my heart the outcome would have most likely been the same. I remembered the doctor's saying David had at least three fatal injuries. This woman had been scared to death. What would I have done? They could have had guns. They were full of rage. They would not have stopped. I had to just resign myself to the fact that no matter what, it had been too late to save him.

Witness after witness testified that they heard David screaming and begging for his life. David Smyth, who lived in a house on Trenton Avenue, where the *actual* party was held that night, testified next. He said Jimmy Galione came back into his home and was bragging. He bragged that the person he hit was unconscious, but he continued to "whack" him anyway. I was furious. Where were this boy's parents? Why did they not call the police? What responsible parent has a houseful of young men out of control and does nothing? These were questions I wanted answered. I think I heard at one point they were not home. I didn't care; I was still holding them partly responsible.

Thomas Ashford worked at a convenience store. He went to school with Jimmy Galione and even played football with him. He testified Galione came into the store right after the incident and was bragging about hitting someone with a hammer. I kept telling myself, *The LORD does not give you more than you can bear. Please, God,* I kept saying, *no more.* I was so close to my breaking point. The words *begging for his life* just echoed around and around in my head. I was beginning to realize David was in pain; he had known they were trying to kill him. He died painfully. This knowledge would have me in pain for the rest of my life.

Joey Weston, Dave's bandmate and one of his closest friends, testified next. Joe was there that night. David was driving him home. He said they did everything they could to get away. He clearly identified Jimmy Galione as the one with the hammer. When asked, he pointed a finger at Galione. He said he would never forget that face. He said he would never forget that big nose.

"We were banging on doors begging for help. Nobody would answer their doors," he said.

He said he saw Dave with his hands up against his face, trying to protect himself. After everyone scattered, Joey testified, they did not see Dave. He ran around looking for him and found him in the driveway. He was bleeding from his nose and his mouth. The side of his head was soaked with blood. Joey said David kept trying to say something. He thought it sounded like Michael. Joe said he sat there holding Dave. Joey was clearly having a tough time testifying. He was crying. He had been a good friend to David. Was he the last person to hear David's voice? He was one of the last people to see David *the way he was.* He was one of the last people to see David as a whole, alive man.

My mind wandered. What were they talking about in the car as David was driving them home? Were they laughing and having a good time? Were they talking about their futures? Were they thinking about work the next day? Perhaps they were talking about their kids. The three of them were new daddies. Did Joe realize that it could have been him lying there in that driveway? I hoped and prayed he realized he was spared for a reason. I hoped he would always remember to be a good and kind person. I prayed that he would never, ever forget David. I hoped he would know he would always be special to me and my family.

I honestly never wondered why God chose David that night. I never did wish it had been Joey or Anthony. I think it would have been perfectly normal to wish it were one of them, but I never did.

Anthony Marino's testimony was next. I could not have pressed my feet any harder into the floor. I knew this was going to be tough.

Anthony was also a bandmate and a best friend to Dave. I always liked Anthony. He'd spent time in my home. He also placed Jimmy Galione with the hammer. I remembered seeing Anthony at the hospital the day after the attack. His face looked as if it had gone through a meat grinder. He said Jimmy Galione had hit him with the hammer. He too cried as he testified. My heart broke for him. He had lost his mother suddenly, and then that *night* happened. Nobody as young as this should have to endure this much pain. I hoped he also knew he was spared for a reason. I hoped he would go on to do something spectacular. I hoped he would be a good father to his little boy, and I prayed he would always be a good friend to Birna and little Michael. I knew if David had lived, there was no doubt they would have been lifelong friends. They could have been grandfathers together, sitting around watching the Eagles and talking about the good ol' days. They could have gone on to become great musicians, perhaps even a very famous band. Thinking about all of these what ifs at this particular moment helped me get through the horror I was hearing and feeling. I thought about the mind and what an amazing thing it was. Then I thought about David's brain, smashed. What kind of a person does that to someone's amazing brain? Why?

The prosecution, I felt, was going well. I have no idea how I lived through the process. I was getting nervous about the defense and what were they going to bring. Would we have to listen to Galione and Reeves get up on the stand and lie? I dreaded having to listen to Mel Kardos. I was so fixated on hating him. I know he was just doing his job. I know every defendant is entitled to representation. I just did not like him. I was really starting to dislike Peter Hall too. They both kept insisting their clients were acting in self-defense, but seven on one is not self-defense. Repeatedly striking someone on the head and body as they are begging for their life is not self-defense. It is murder. Witness after witness testified that David was begging for his life, lying on the ground. These witnesses had no reason to lie. They did not want to be there. The truth has no agenda. They did not choose to see or hear what happened that night. It made me angry every time I heard the word *self-defense*. I wanted to hear, *We went out looking for a fight. We found one, and we went too far.* I just wanted them to tell the truth. I wanted them to be sorry.

I was still confused about what actually happened at the police station that night. I know Joe and Anthony were there the entire night. Randy told me he had them there the entire night. I heard testimony that Jimmy Galione had been back to the party house, given by Mark Cupitt. He was also seen in a convenience store by Thomas Ashford. It was obvious he was not at the police station all night. I wondered if the police testimony would answer some of these questions for me. My main question was still how much longer we would have to wait for more arrests. I was still waiting patiently for that to happen. I was obsessed with the fact that they were out there, free to live their lives. The waiting was physically painful.

Officer Joe Moors took the stand and recounted the interview he had with Jerry Reeves that night. He said Reeves admitted to whacking Dave over the head with the level more than once. He admitted to me he "just went crazy." Officer Moors said that Jerry appeared remorseful. At that time, David had not died. He was still in the hospital, fighting for his life. *That* night, the police had no idea how severe Dave's injuries were.

Moors testified that Galione showed up at the police station in the early morning with his parents. Moors said Galione appeared upset. He testified that Jimmy Galione admitted to him that he had hit David in the head with the hammer. Galione told Police Detective Randy Morris he hit the guy in the side of the head with the hammer. The guy yelled and then fell face down in the driveway.

I felt sick again. I wanted to scream, "Why did you keep hitting him?" I remembered the doctor saying the blow to the side of David's face was only *one* of the fatal blows. He also testified that Jimmy Galione asked how much time he would get for hitting the guy with the hammer. Mel Kardos kept saying the "hammer" was a red herring. I was so sick of listening to him. There was another hammer somewhere. I wanted to scream, "It's in the Delaware River, you idiots."

Officer Brian Detrick testified next. He was with David in the driveway as they waited for the ambulance. I had heard he was very disturbed by what he saw that night. He seemed so young. He said he knew the person was hurt badly. David had been unresponsive.

# THIRD DAY OF TRIAL

The days just seemed to be running into one another. I would go home at night and just lay in my bed, replaying everything in my mind I'd heard that day. I tried keeping a journal. We were getting very close to the end of the prosecution's case. What I was seeing and hearing was awful enough. I tried to prepare myself mentally for how much worse it was going to be.

The DNA evidence was so confusing. There were so many numbers. I hate math. The experts were testifying that Jimmy Galione's DNA was not on the hammer that belonged to Dave. They also said none of Galione's DNA was found on Dave. That made sense to me, and I hoped it made sense to the jury. If Galione was hitting David with *another* hammer, and David was lying on the ground unable to defend himself, of course they would not find Galione's DNA on Dave. The real question was whether Galione had Dave's DNA on him. That we do not know, because Galione showed up at the police station the following morning, showered.

Jerry Reeves's DNA was found on the level. Reeves's public defender's explanation was that Jerry was hit with the level. If I had not been so devastated, this would have been funny. There was a lot of arguing between the DNA experts. It was difficult to keep up.

Dr. Ian Hood, forensic pathologist, was the next to testify. His opinion was that David died from blunt force trauma. Dr. Hood described in detail twelve injuries. There were two holes in David's skull, multiple fractures on his nose, multiple cheek fractures, multiple fractures around his ears, three broken ribs, and a fractured vertebra. Birna ran out of the courtroom in tears as Dr. Hood showed the jury autopsy photos of these injuries. I do not know how I stayed. I just wanted to know about every injury. I wanted to link each injury with *someone*—the vicious, scumbag, excuse-for-a-human-being *someone*—responsible. Dr. Hood stated that the facial injuries were consistent with Dave's head being repeatedly slammed onto a hard surface, such as a concrete driveway. Other injuries were consistent with being struck by a rectangular-shaped object, the level.

Matt then entered into evidence the confessions. The defense attorneys did their best to have these thrown out. In his confession, written in his own handwriting the morning after the murder, Jimmy Galione wrote that he struck David with the hammer. He wrote that he struck him more than once. Listening to these animals' own words was chilling, to say the least. It was no wonder their attorneys wanted the confessions thrown out. They told the truth.

There was nothing on earth that could have ever prepared me for what we were to hear next. Our NOVA advocates tried to tell us this would be the hardest part of the trial. Matt played the 911 tapes for the jury. I believe there were close to ninety of them. Loretta was screaming, "They are killing him!" Neighbor after neighbor pleaded for help. They tried. From what we could piece together, the police responded quickly. They arrived within minutes. It was just so confusing. There were so many people running. On many of the 911 tapes, people reported hearing gunfire. This caused the police to react a bit slower. I tried to imagine the scene in my mind and just come up with chaos. By the time the medical team reached David, Jimmy Galione was washing blood off of his hands, and Jerry Reeves was high fiving his friends on another corner.

That was the end of the prosecution. In my mind, there was *no* defense. I believed the prosecution proved their case—David's case—beyond a shadow of doubt. I screamed the whole forty-minute ride home that day. The pain of actually hearing Dave's voice on those tapes was unbearable. I was emotionally out of control. I wanted to crash my car into a bridge. I kept seeing Allyson's face and kept trying to remember my promise to make something good come out of this horror. I had no idea how I would ever manage this, but I had to.

# THE DEFENSE BEGINS

The mood in the hallway of the courthouse was different this morning. As far as my family, we all looked as if we were zombies. We were only there because we *had* to be. The other side, the murderer's family and friends, were buzzing around like spring had just sprung. They were all smiles with one another and all evil glares for us. We filed into the courtroom unable to avoid bumping elbows with *the enemies.* God help me, I hated them—all of the murderers' family and friends. I wished horror on them all.

Mel Kardos called Detective Randy Morris to the stand. Kardos accused Randy of arresting the wrong man. He then accused Morris of not wanting to admit he'd arrested the wrong man because the arrest had been in the paper.

"You did not want to look stupid," he shouted at Morris. He also claimed his client's arrest was politically motivated because the police chief, Frank Peranteau, was running for a vacant district justice seat. How Detective Morris managed to stay calm is beyond me. He remained impressively calm and confident.

He continued to claim his client was not involved in or responsible for David's death. Where was he when his client's confession was entered as evidence? Kardos suggested Reeves was arrested three weeks later because Morris knew he had the wrong guy. He accused Morris of not wanting to look like a "dope." This went on for two awful hours. While Kardos continued to *shout* question after question, Morris calmly responded. Morris stated that he was certain, when the brawl was over, there was only one man lying injured in a driveway. He also stated that Galione admitted and wrote down in his statement to police that he hit a man with a hammer and the man fell down in a driveway.

Kardos then put Jimmy Galione's girlfriend, Janine Poloio, on the stand. She was the girl that had been terrorizing Birna. She said Galione came home that night and changed his clothes. She admitted she washed his clothes. There was only one reason I could imagine she would be doing laundry at two in the morning. She was trying to wash away her boyfriend's guilt. I remember thinking, *As soon as Galione goes to prison, this girl will be history.* I had heard rumors Galione had been very abusive toward her. I believed it was probably true. Nonetheless, she should have been arrested for tampering with evidence. Why did this not happen? She got away with a crime. I hoped every time the Galiones used their washer, they thought about the innocent blood that went down their drain. I wished horrible affliction to Janine Poloio. I hoped for the rest of her life, she would dream of having David's blood on her hands.

Mr. Galione, Jimmy's father, testified next. He looked awful. He looked to me like he had been drinking a lot. He testified that his son did not own and was not wearing a red sweatshirt. Loretta Mulkiewicz testified that the man who was hitting David in her driveway was wearing a red sweatshirt. I almost passed out when Matt pulled out a photo that had been taken at the police station that morning. The photo depicted Jimmy Galione clearly wearing a red sweatshirt. Oohs and ahhs went through the courtroom. Randy testified that the police routinely take photos of all involved in fights. The photographs are usually used to document injuries. Jimmy Galione had no injuries. I felt a wave of relief over my body. Matt had proven that at least Jimmy Galione was guilty. The elder Galione was caught in a lie. He should have been charged. I made a mental note to discuss that with Matt.

Steve Owtscharuk was next to take the stand. He said David started the fight. I could have laughed at that statement. David never started a fight in his life. That was just a fact. He said someone in the car said, "These guys want to fight." Steve testified he took off his hat and removed his earring. That convinced me this was not his first street fight. He then testified that David, Joey, and Anthony came at them with the hammer, the level, and a broomstick. He claimed he was beaten, Jim Williams had been beaten, and Jerry Reeves had been beaten with the level. The police produced photos of each of them. They did not have so much as a bruise on them.

I felt sick again. I remembered it was Steve who had supposedly ripped Michael's car seat out of the car. I hated him. I studied the jurors' faces. I wondered if they were convinced that what Steve was saying was true. It was hard to tell; they were all so serious. My guess was that they were listening intently and did not believe one word Steve was saying. David, Anthony, and Joey were big men. They were also in great shape. They were also older and much more mature. They were family men. The truth is, if David had hit Jerry Reeves with that level, Jerry would be the one who was dead. It was just that plain and simple. If Anthony or Joey had hit any of them with one of these weapons, that person also would have been severely injured or dead. David, Joey, and Anthony were the ones who were ambushed. They were running for their lives. It could not have happened any other way.

I saw no proof of any injuries to any of these guys—a few scratches, maybe. David was an extremely passive man, and it would have taken a lot for him to even fight back. He never had a chance.

Kardos then called John Scancella to the stand. I had known this boy since he was a baby. He was one of my son's best friends. He was also a close friend to Jimmy Galione. He was cousin to my son-in-law, Dominic. I knew his parents well and liked them. He was also the same boy who signed up to join the army with my son and then left him stranded. The rumor back then was that his father pressured him not to go. The rumor was that Vince, John's father, was practically forcing him to testify for Galione. Why would Vince do that? I never understood the justification. I also never understood the weakness of John. He should have stood up and been his own man. I felt the whole Scancella family took a knife and put it straight through my heart and twisted it; the hurt was unbearable.

My sister was beside herself with anger. My daughter, Jill, was devastated; she'd really liked John. It really scared me to believe that people could look at the facts here and believe it was anything more than cold-blooded murder. I am a strong believer in karma and was convinced that, for this choice, the Scancella family would be struck with some *really* bad karma. I am not an evil person, but I do know the difference between right and wrong, and there was nothing right about what happened to David. There was also no right in *lying* for a murderer. John sat on that witness stand and told the jury Jimmy Galione was a stand-up, all around nice guy. He also said he never knew him to be violent.

Kardos then put medical experts on the stand. He was trying to insinuate David had been drinking and doing drugs that night. That claim was quickly shot down. Experts testified David had less than a half beer in his system and no drugs. I recalled asking the doctor in the emergency room that night if they did blood work. I had a feeling it might be important. Dave was not a big drinker, nor did he do drugs. He was working that night. He had been preparing for a big show.

Kardos also tried to get the jury to believe that David's injuries had been caused by a fall. Peter Hall was still insisting his client was acting in self-defense. Mel Kardos was still insisting his client never hit David. I kept thinking how much easier this would be on everyone if the truth were just told.

Kardos then paraded a handful of witnesses who said that Jimmy Galione was always just a nice, polite young man with a bright future. Matt answered with his own witnesses who testified to seeing Galione strike his girlfriend and other witnesses who testified he was always looking for a fight. My daughter, Jillian, was one of those witnesses. She was just eighteen, and I could not have been more proud of her. She did not let Kardos rattle her at all. She remained focused and told the truth.

With that, the defense was finished. I took a deep breath and thanked God I made it through the horrific details. Some questions I had answered, but I still had so many more.

# CLOSING ARGUMENTS

A surprise snowstorm the next morning caused a four-hour delay to the start of closing arguments. I kept telling myself it was almost over. I was confident that Matt and the police had proven beyond the shadow of a doubt that Galione and Reeves were guilty of murdering David. I was quite sure Peter Hall did not prove Jerry Reeves acted in self-defense. I was more than positive Mel Kardos did not prove Jimmy Galione was innocent.

I thought about the jury. We were getting close to the time when they would have to decide. I hoped they had heard everything I heard. I prayed for them and their families.

The snow was beautiful, but the delay seemed endless. The hallway outside the courtroom was crowded. It seemed everyone in Bucks County was anxious to hear the closing arguments. The media was there in full force. I just sat on a bench and prayed.

The courtroom doors were opened, and once again, like cattle, the large group squeezed through the double doors and found a seat.

It was noisy. Everybody was talking. I could not wait for the judge to walk in and shut everyone up.

Mel Kardos started giving his closing argument. Actually, what he did was give an hour-long speech in which he quoted Shakespeare, the Bible, Mark Twain, and Socrates. He said Galione's only involvement in the fight was wrestling the hammer out of David's hands. He accused the police of framing his client in order to have a speedy arrest. He claimed the police knew they had the wrong man. I thought he would never shut up.

Peter Hall stated once again his client acted only in self-defense. He pointed to the testimony of Steve Owtscharuk. He said Dave and his buddies started the fight. He accused Joey and Anthony of lying because they wanted someone to pay for Dave's death. He said the police were "overwhelmed" by this case. He claimed Jerry Reeves was "treated differently" by the police and not given the same opportunity as the other suspects. I froze when I heard that statement. Peter Hall, I really hoped, was not going to make this about race. He tried.

David was not there to defend himself. He was not given the opportunity to defend himself *that night*. Jerry had his chance to defend himself. He should have just told the truth. He should not have been driving around looking for someone to beat up, *that night* or any other night. He should have been being a father to his baby daughter. He should not have been whining, *Poor me, I am being picked on because of my race.* Peter Hall should be embarrassed for even uttering those words. It sounded like he was desperate. Peter Hall then asked the jury to find the witnesses who testified against his client to be found not credible. That would be *all* the neighbors on Wilson Avenue, Reeves's own friends, and Joey and Anthony. I'd tried to like Peter Hall before then. Now I hated him too. What a scumbag.

Matt's closing argument was emotional, to say the least. He asked the jury to use common sense. He reminded them of the testimony of neighbor after neighbor stating that David was lying on the ground, begging for his life as he was being beaten with a hammer and kicked in the head. He reminded the jurors that David's skull was nearly split in half. He slammed a photo of David down on the defense table in front of Galione and Reeves and said, "This was not self-defense; it was murder!" Everyone in the courtroom, including me, jumped. Matt asked the jury to consider third-degree murder and explained to them that meant a *willful and malicious act, not necessarily pre-meditated*. A third-degree-murder conviction carries a twenty-to-forty-year sentence. I wanted first-degree murder. I believed they set out to kill *someone* that night. I believe David was tortured mercilessly. Unfortunately, our justice system is not that simple. It is very complicated.

God bless Matt; his closing argument was dramatic, and he shook us out of our seats, but he got right to the point. He did not drag it out ridiculously. He made no excuses. It was over.

# IN THE JURY'S HANDS

It was up to the jury. Justice for David and his family was up to these twelve brave strangers. I wished I could hear them deliberate. I had to trust them. I had no choice. The judge gave the jury long, drawn-out instructions, and the jury left the courtroom. We would wait.

My son's wife was having contractions. I hoped my new grandbaby would hold off until the jury made their decision. I was anxious to meet this new life. It was the only thing getting me through this nightmare. It was like the proverbial light at the end of the tunnel. David would have been so happy for my son. He should be here. I did want someone to pay. I wanted them all to pay. I wanted them to pay with their lives. Not that I wanted them to die—I would not want their families to suffer the way we have; I just wanted them in jail for a long time—a very, very long time behind bars, suffering and haunted by David's voice begging for his life. I never wanted them to know the joy of a new child.

The waiting was agonizing. I walked the halls of the courthouse. I stared out the window. I talked with my kids. Galione's family was glaring at us. For the life of me, I could not understand why they hated us. Where was their empathy? Where was their shame? I had once felt sorry for them. I thought they were good people and did not deserve to be going through any of this. I just did not get why they were so cruel.

The jury had not made a decision. They asked the judge to be excused for the night. I remembered from watching television shows that the longer the jury deliberated, the worse the news is for the prosecution. It was so hard to watch Galione and Reeves walk out of that courthouse. They were both free on bail. The thought of them at home with their families made me crazy. I could only hope the next day would be the day we would witness the two of them led off to prison in shackles.

It was such a long night. I could not sleep. I wondered if that would be the night the baby would enter the world. I prayed God would let us hear the verdict first. I prayed for the baby's health. I prayed for Birna and little Michael. He looked so much like David it frightened me sometimes. I thought about the day he was born. I was so lucky to have been there. I will never forget the look of relief on David's face and his gorgeous smile as he admired his wife and baby son. I started to cry. Did I ever thank David for inviting me to be there that day? I was sure he knew, but did I ever actually tell him? I would remember to tell Birna. I needed her to know how important that day was to me. It was the first time I actually saw a baby born except for my own babies.

It was hard to get up that next morning. My eyes were swollen from crying all night. I looked awful, and I did not care. I was freezing. I pulled myself together and drove to the courthouse. I was so sick of the long ride. I was sick and tired of the long walk from the parking lot to the courthouse. It was so wrong that they closed the entrance doors closest to the parking lot. You had to walk all the way around this huge, round building to the front doors.

They had installed metal detectors, and I guess it was too expensive to install the security at both entrances. People have no common sense. Why would they not install the security at the door where most of the people entered the courthouse? I made my way up the stairs and sat on a bench. I looked around. My brother Frank was lying on a bench. Reporters were asking questions and taking pictures. Our NOVA advocates were there. They explained to us what would happen once there was a verdict. They were so comforting. I had no idea what we would have done without their knowledge of the system and their tissues. I hoped I could do the same one day for someone. I wanted to be that kind of a person. I looked over at the police chief; he was pacing. Was he nervous? I started to panic. Would it be possible the jury could find them not guilty? What would I do if that happened? What would we all do? I spoke with Mia, our court advocate. I told her how scared I was. She told me she felt strongly there would be a guilty verdict. She also said you could never tell with a jury. Strange things could happen.

We decided to eat in shifts so we would not miss the announcement that the jury had a decision. I could not even think about food, but I thought the cold air on my face might wake me up a little. The walk across the street to Maxwell's was a chilly one.

Everybody had an opinion as to why the jury took so long. Some thought it was a good sign; others thought it could be a bad sign.

I thought about the insanity of the victim's family and the accused family's right there together in this hallway. It was absurd. There should certainly be special rooms made available for victims and their families. I found this whole set up to be cruel and unusual. I made a mental note to try to change that. I tried lying on the bench to sleep. It was so uncomfortable. My brother Nick was pacing. How would he ever get past it? I wanted to take him into my arms and tell him it would all be okay. However, I knew it never would be okay.

I must have drifted off to sleep and was awakened by people who started to mumble loudly and walk around. Several Bucks County sheriff's deputies appeared in the hallway. Something was happening. They were setting up a metal detection device at the courtroom door. I saw a friendly face. Sam the policeman, a former Bristol Borough police officer, was now a sheriff. We had been friends for years. He told me it would be a first-come, first-serve basis getting into the courtroom. I immediately got into the line and made sure my family joined me.

After fifteen hours of deliberation, the jury had a verdict. I could not catch my breath. The sheriffs questioned and searched everyone entering the courtroom. They told us we had to refrain from any outburst once the verdicts were read. We were also told we had to remain in our seats. I walked in and took my seat. I got as close to the front of the courtroom and the jury as I could. I was squeezing my court advocate's hand as hard as I could. The judge was talking, but I could not hear what he was saying. I really felt like I was going to pass out. Somebody was yelling "Quiet!" I think she was called the bailiff. She actually gave me dirty looks. I was so exhausted and frustrated. I wished she would stop trying to catch me chewing gum. She was the gum and cell phone police of the courtroom. God help you if she caught you with either. She needed a lesson in empathy for victims. I could just tell she assumed that if you were in a courtroom, you were a bad person. On the other hand, perhaps it was just a major power trip. I hated her!

The jury walked in and took their seats. I looked at every one of their faces. They looked confident and relieved. Was that a good sign? The little piece of paper with their decision was carried to the judge.

"In the matter of the state against Jerry Reeves…" The judge read the charges and then said "guilty" after each one of the charges. I was trembling, shaking uncontrollably. I heard Jerry's mother sobbing loudly. I looked over at Birna; she was crying. I looked over at the jury, smiled, and mouthed *thank you*. The witch bailiff was shouting "Quiet!" again.

"In the matter of the state against Jimmy Galione..." the judge said, "murder, not guilty."

I was going to be sick. I wanted to scream. I sat there frozen. He continued to read down the list of charges. When he got to conspiracy and said "guilty," his family started to scream.

I remember his sister, Angela, shouting, "Why are they doing this to him?" I wanted to punch her in her face. Her brother did this to himself. David was dead because of him. At the same time, I was confused; I did not understand why they were so upset over conspiracy. My court advocate just squeezed my hand and said it was good. She said the conspiracy charge carries the same weight as murder. I was so relieved. It was finally over.

I gave Matt, the police officers, and the chief hugs. I hugged my family. Jimmy Galione was wiping his eyes. Jerry Reeves showed no emotion. Their families were crying. Janine Poloio tried to run from the courtroom, but the deputies stopped her. As mean as it sounds, I got pleasure out of her anguish. Nicole Rivera, Jerry Reeves's girlfriend, was sobbing. They had been so mean to my family. Justice felt good. Matt told us they would be sentenced to no less than fifteen years and up to as much as forty years. The sentencing would happen in a few weeks. Defendants must be sentenced within sixty days; it is their *right* to have a speedy trial and sentencing.

I got to witness what I had waited so long to see. The deputies handcuffed them and led them out of the courtroom and off to prison. The judge ordered their bail revoked. The defense attorneys were still arguing over bail being revoked. They both vowed to appeal. I did not even want to think about what any of that meant. I just wanted to feel relieved. The jury was thanked by the judge and released. I mouthed *thank you* and *God bless you* to them again. I felt better than I had in months. Chief Paranteau assured us more arrests would be possible now. The deputies wanted the three families to leave the courtroom separately. We were told to remain seated. *Yeah,* I thought, *make the victim's family sit there longer.* We should have been able to leave first. The others could have very easily waited in the parking lot for us. We just spent the time thanking Matt, the police officers, and our advocates for their dedication in seeking justice for David.

It was finally time to go home. I walked outside looked up at the sky and smiled to Dave. It started to snow. Marlana, my son's wife, was in labor, and as a family, we were all headed to the hospital. My new grandchild had perfect timing.

Bottom, from right: Mom, Joanie, Nicky. Top, from right: David, Frankie, Doreen. Newport, RI, 1976.

Nicky, Newport, RI, 1976.

David and Joanie, 1978.

The Bookends: David, Frank, Nick, Denise, Doreen, 1988.

Alyssa and Renee, 1997

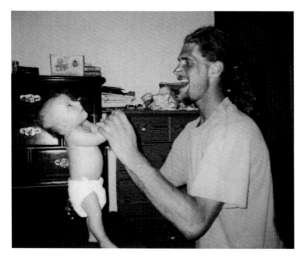

David and Michael, 1998.

Cheryl, Alexis, and Frank, 2000.

Baby Tony (He's 21 now and still Baby Tony!) and Michael, 2001.

Right: Michael, 2001.
Below: Dominic, 2002.

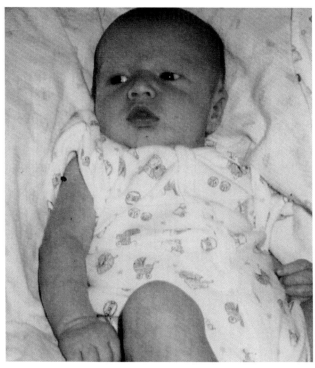

Allyson, 2002.

Jimmy and Julia, 2004.

Ryan, 2006.

*This day I will marry my best friend......The one I laugh with, live for, dream with...love.*

*John McGettigan & Doreen Brinkerhoff would be honored to have you share in our happiness on Sunday June 17, 2007 at 7:15 in the evening on the beach at the end of Sumner Street in Strathmere, New Jersey.*

*The celebration will continue immediately following the ceremony at 101 Randolph Street, Strathmere, NJ.*

*Please RSVP to John at 610-659-4390 by May 20, 2007*

*Children are welcome!!*

John and Doreen's wedding invitation, 2007.

Bottom, from left: Jimmy, Michael, Julia, Avery, Dominic, Morgan. Top, from left: John, Doreen, Allyson, 2007.

Doreen, John, and families, 2007.

NOVA's Ecumenical Service; Victim's Memorial Arbor and Gazebo; Core Creek Park; Langhorne, PA; 2008.

# POST TRIAL

Doylestown's origins dated back to 1745, when William Doyle obtained a license to build a tavern on the corner of Main and State Streets. The strategic location to Philadelphia made it an ideal area for a village. In 1838, the borough of Doylestown was incorporated. It reminded me of Bristol. The streets even had the same names. The difference was right in the middle of the town: this huge, round building that just never seemed to belong there; it was too modern. Surrounded by old row houses and strips of old storefronts, the building looked obnoxious.

I turned and gave the round, ugly building one last glance and got into my car. It was beginning to snow really hard. How ironic it was that my son's baby would be born on *this* day. Another prayer answered. I had asked God to hold off until the verdict was read.

What an extreme range of emotions I should have had at that time. In my now-all-too-familiar dream state, all I felt was numb. I was still in shock. I thanked God the jury had made the right decision. I was definitely not happy, but I was relieved the verdicts were guilty. The jury did their job. The prosecution did their job. The witnesses bravely did their part. Now it was up to the judge.

Our NOVA advocates explained to us that the judge gave the sentences, and they explained the process. I had no doubt these animals were going to prison for a very long time.

I wondered how bad the roads would be and opted for the turnpike. Would I make it to the hospital in time? I wondered if the baby was a boy or a girl. I really did like to know beforehand. It seemed like there was more bonding. At any rate, I just prayed Marlana and the baby would both be healthy.

I was rushing through the hospital doors and hoping I had not missed the moment. I looked around the waiting room. Everyone was there. My daughters, my sister, my brothers, and Marlana's family were all there. The only one missing from this moment was David. Would I ever stop missing him? I was quickly informed that my son was feeling very sick, had a fever, and would not be allowed to be with his wife. It was up to her mother, Patty, and me. The nurses assured us they would bring my son in at the last minute, and he would be able to witness the birth from a distance. I was worried about my son. Was it the flu? Was it his nerves? He looked awful. I went in and took my place to the right of Marlana. Her mom had her left hand. I looked out of the big window in the room; the snow was still falling. After what seemed like hours of pushing, on January 24, 2000, baby girl Brinkerhoff was born. She had the biggest blue eyes and white hair (very little hair). She was gorgeous. I could not stop looking at her. She looked just like her daddy had when he was born. I was so relieved everyone was okay. My son was feeling better, his wife looked radiant, and the baby was healthy. She had no name yet.

I was tired. I wondered if years from now I would remember this night just like it was yesterday. Would I remember the trial and think, *Has it been that long?* I had a hard time falling asleep. I did not have to get up and go to the courthouse. I just had to get up and go see a beautiful, brand new life that God seemed to send at just the right time. I dozed on and off throughout the night. Little snippets of statements I had heard in court, glimpses of the horrific photographs seen throughout the trial, the verdict, and the anxiety of waiting for the trial to be over played out in my dreams. Whenever I was shaken awake, I remembered the tiny little miracle waiting for her mom-mom to hold her.

It snowed all night. My car was completely covered, and my driveway seemed a mile long. The plow guy said he would not be able to get there, well, until he got there. I wanted to see the baby. I called the hospital. Jimmy and Marlana were going round and round, trying to come up with a name. It *had* to be a name that started with a J. I made my suggestions, and by late afternoon, it was decided. Her name was Julia Sierra.

It was surreal being stuck in the house. It really was strange to not be rushing to get to court on time. I was not worrying about the sentencing; I knew it had to be at least twenty years. I wanted life, but I convinced myself I would be satisfied with twenty-five years. I just never considered it would be anything less. My thoughts went to the others: *when would they be arrested?* I imagined the relief I would feel when I got the news.

I went back to work again and once again felt like I'd walked into a planet that had just kept on moving while I was stuck on another planet. I was told there would be something called a pre-sentencing investigation. I had to figure out what that meant, and it was nothing more than another little matter to cause me anxiety.

My inability to concentrate caused me to make mistakes at work. I did not want to be there. I had to be because I was broke. I never thought about the financial burden that *crime* placed on a family. I wondered how I would ever be caught up with bills. Just another *little thing* to cause anxiety. I tried not to think about money.

The Saturday after the trial ended, I went to a local diner for lunch. It was called the Golden Dawn and was at Five Points in Levittown. It had been there forever—well, as long as I could remember. The booths were separated by glass. I happened to glance over at another booth and saw one of the jurors. I don't know why I was shocked. Where did I think these jurors came from, New Jersey? Of course they came from Bucks County, and of course it was possible I could run into them. I had an overwhelming need to go over and say something. I wanted to say thank you, at least, but I was nervous. I had spent weeks being told not to look at them and to never say a word to them. I got up and walked over. The man recognized me immediately. He got emotional, and so did I. He said it was one of the hardest things he ever had to do. He asked me questions about my family members, I thanked him, and that was that. I did not even ask his name. Why did I not ask? Now I wanted to run into all of them. Everywhere I went, I looked.

We had to deal with a pre-sentencing investigation. The investigator wanted to talk to our whole family, so we all met with her at my brother Nick's house. She was the investigator for Jerry Reeves. She explained that she would do interviews with both sides and then give her opinion to the judge. We told her what we knew about Jerry. We told her about him hitting his girlfriend's father over the head with a frying pan, but the man dropped the charges. I suddenly hated that man. Perhaps if he had followed through, Jerry would have been in jail and David would still be alive. She asked us how we felt about what had happened to Dave. How did she think we felt?

I realized I was starting to have real feelings of anger. I had been angry but in a numb way. I knew I was *supposed* to be angry, so I acted angry. I had never been an *angry* person. I don't know when it started, but I was an expert at calm, cool, and collected. Now I could feel my body actually get warm whenever I thought about Dave and the people involved in killing him. It scared me. It did not help that I did not like this investigator. She did not appear at all interested in us or our feelings. I could just imagine the meeting she would have with Jerry's family—his mother crying, his girlfriend pleading; I wanted to gag just thinking about that scene.

I thought again about taking some medication as my doctor suggested but again decided against taking anything. I knew if I had half a chance of coming out on the other side of this nightmare with any shred of sanity, I needed to deal with my feelings.

We heard from NOVA that Jimmy Galione waived his right to his pre-sentencing investigation. I wondered why. This made me angry, and I did not even know why. Did he have something to hide?

*Of course he does,* I thought.

Maybe he was worried about what my kids would say about him. On the other hand, and even better, maybe he was afraid of what his own family and friends would say about him. I hoped it would make no difference at the sentencing. Matt told us Mel Kardos was going to do his own study. I'm sure he charged for that. Matt told us Kardos believed the investigations often favored the prosecution. He told us not to worry.

The memorial site on Wilson Avenue and East Circle became a symbol of Dave and a place I visit often. I felt cheated because I had no grave to visit. I was so amazed whenever I stopped at the memorial sight on Wilson Avenue. The neighbors would come out and tell me how frightened they felt *that* night and how they wished they could have done more.

I had been told by our court advocates that the grieving process for people in my situation really cannot even begin until all of the legal proceedings have ended. Perhaps that's why I've begun to feel so angry. We are getting close to *the end* of the proceedings. I remembered the five stages of grief: denial, anger, bargaining, depression, and acceptance. My advocate suggested I start attending a grief support group. I decided I would do that after the sentencing.

I was thinking about how differently everyone in this family was handling or not handling grief. Joan was angry and sad. Her own husband, Dominic, had been born and raised in Bristol. He knew all of these people. He was torn.

My son was hiding his feelings. He had a new baby girl and just seemed to want to move on with his life. He had no idea that he would have to deal with *his* feelings eventually. Sometimes I just wanted to scream at him, "These were your friends that did this! Why are you not freaking out?" Jill was angry. She felt betrayed by the people she grew up with and thought she knew. She was so young—they all were—to have to deal with this pain. I just wanted to make it all go away for them, but I couldn't. I had to find a way to fix *me* first. I had to find a way to go on.

Birna seemed to be going out a lot. People were talking about her, and it made me so angry. I could not be in her shoes and I would *never, ever* judge her for anything she did. I really wanted to be there for her, to take care of her and Michael and tell her everything would be okay. I really wanted to; I just couldn't.

My sister's kids were having trouble in school. Her daughter, Renee, had to be in school every day with Jerry Reeves's younger sister. The school seemed to be divided. Why wouldn't it be? The whole town was divided. For me, it was as simple as right or wrong, and those who chose the wrong side, well, I believed in karma. My brother Frank was hurting really badly. I could *feel* him hurting. I was so relieved he had Cheryl in his life, because he certainly did not have me. I was incapable. My brother Nick was not even on my radar. He was angry with me. He said I wasn't really even his sister. He said David was the only sibling he had. He was angry, and I understood. I forgave him. I just wanted to know that he was okay. It was just such a dark hole for all of us. I just told myself to give it time.

I was not sure if I was grieving or if I was doing it correctly. I am such a technical thinker sometimes. A lot of people had opinions, but I needed a plan, a list of steps I could cross off one by one. I knew I had to do this so I would not screw up the rest of my life. I wondered if I even wanted to *have* a rest of my life. If David was in such a better place, maybe I wanted to be there too so he wouldn't have to be alone. Whenever I started to feel this way, there was Allyson's chubby little face. She loved me so much. I could not leave her. She was still waiting for the airplane to bring Uncle David back from heaven. "Jesus fixed Uncle David's head, and now he is sending him home." I didn't even know how to explain any of this to her.

I kept convincing myself I needed time. I needed to feel this way. I had to go through this process so I could move on. I started to hate the word *time*. Time was my enemy. It was always there, and it just did not move fast enough. I was waiting for the sentencing hearing to be over and behind us. I was waiting for the right time to join a counseling group. I was waiting for my job or my boss to get better because I was starting to hate my time there. I was waiting to feel happy again, and yet the thought of feeling happy made me feel guilty.

One day I banged my head on my kitchen cabinet. It stung and brought tears to my eyes. I felt so guilty for crying over such a little bump. Poor David's skull was practically smashed in two, and I was whining about a little bump. That was the end of that. I would never complain about a little pain again, ever. I needed time, so I would just wait.

I continued to dwell on and try to find the missing pieces of what actually happened *that night*. I thought again about the term *gang mentality*. What exactly did that mean? How could someone stop it from happening? I wanted to know who made the phone call for the second car that night. Did that car just happen upon Jerry's car? Was it Jerry Reeves? Was he the gang leader? Had he been disrespected during the first fight—the fight he went looking for and started? Did he make a call, and his homeboys came running? None of them wanted to lose respect because Bristol boyz always stick together! Antonio and Mark were the only two that ran away. Why was that? What in them made them realize *that particular* fight was out of control? Was it their family life? Were their parents there for them when they needed an identity? Were they recognized at home for being good at *something?* Why did they have ethical values and the others had none? Jimmy Galione came from a good family; at least, it appeared that way. His father was a good ol' Bristol boy. Is it possible that some people are just born evil? Was this the case with him? I remembered a time when Jimmy Galione's little sister Michelle was at our house playing Barbies with Jill. I remembered him purposely stepping on her hand, hard.

Jerry Reeves's parents were not together and obviously had not worked together to raise their son. He had obviously had anger issues for years. The others, I believe, just went along because they had nothing to stand for, no values. They had no empathy.

I knew one thing for sure. That *incident,* David's death, was tearing the tiny town of Bristol apart. It was discussed everywhere. They were talking about it in the Wawa, the diners, the churches, and the bars. Everybody had an opinion. There were actually people that believed David's death was an unfortunate accident and chalked it up to "boys will be boys." They did not believe those guys were killers. I wanted to scream at the top of my lungs. Those are the types of people who believe if a mother drowns her kids, it's *oops, terrible unfortunate mistake.* They would feel sorry for a guy who raped and say the poor thing did not have enough toys or attention when he was little and he did not mean to hurt that girl. Thank God for the people who believed it was wrong to beat an innocent man to death. Thank God the jury did not buy in to any of this. Thank God *most* people value human life and know the difference between right and wrong. Personally, I would have been fine with never stepping foot in that town again. My kids, however, where standing their ground; they would not let those killers take their hometown from them.

The sentencing date was getting close. Our court advocates told us we had the right to give an impact statement at the hearing. We would tell the judge how this crime had impacted our lives and would continue to affect our future. I began working on mine two weeks before the sentencing. We had to hand them into the judge so he could read them prior to the hearing. That seemed a little ridiculous to me; wouldn't that take the impact out of the statement? I wrote and rewrote my statement. I prayed for the strength to be able to read it without falling apart. I was filled with anxiety and fear.

# THE SENTENCING

Driving to the courthouse that day was surreal. I could not believe it was March 17, 2000. It was Saint Patrick's Day. Hopefully, that meant the day would be *lucky*. But what I wanted had nothing to do with luck and everything to do with justice.

David died in April. It was nearly a year later. I had trouble comprehending it had almost been a year. Michael turned two that March. I thought about Michael's first birthday. That was the last time our entire family was together, happy. I remembered Dave's smile that day as he proudly held his son. The tears started.

I had to pull over. I had to pull myself together. I wanted to do an effective job reading my impact statement. The prosecutor told us it was *our* day in court. We did not have to cry quietly. We were not going to be told where we could look and where we couldn't. *Our day* in court. Yes, that was important. I had to get myself together.

I pulled down my visor mirror and did my best to repair my running makeup. Shortly, I would witness once again the two scumbags being led to prison in shackles, but this time it would be for at least twenty-five years. That thought gave me peace—not happiness, just peace. I could not help that feeling. The thought of the two of them being thrown into little cells with little windows, alone—God forgive me, but that was satisfying. I felt better, stronger, so I pulled back onto the road.

As I saw the huge, round building, I thought about how out of place it looked in this old town. It was too modern. I wondered who designed the ugly building. Maybe ugly isn't fair; it didn't fit the landscape of historic Doylestown. Supposedly, the courthouse was built there because Doylestown was the center of Bucks County. I wondered what it looked like from the air. It probably looked like a big, round, ugly dot right there in the center of Bucks County.

I loved the quaint little town. The shops, old Victorian homes, galleries, restaurants, and of course the bars and churches that reminded me of Bristol. Many of the people that lived in this town were stuck up. They thought their town was better than Bristol. They thought *they* were better people, but they did not have the Delaware River, and I doubted that town could even come close to the *real* small-town feel of Bristol.

Once again, there were many sheriffs in the hallway leading to the courtroom. I was surprised by the large crowd. I scanned around, looking for my family. I did not feel safe with so many people gathered in such a small area. I saw my friend Sam, the policeman. I would have to remember to wish him a happy Saint Patrick's Day. I knew it was one of his favorites. I missed seeing him in his patrol car in Bristol. He had been there for so long.

I was bombarded by my family with the news that Galione and Reeves also had the right to have people speak on their behalves. I was livid. We should have known. It would have changed the way we prepared. We would have had more letters written; we would have asked more friends and relatives to be here for us. I tried so hard not to cry. I did not want to have to fix my makeup again. I wanted to appear confident and in control.

I was truly shocked to see that Nicole Rivera, Jerry Reeves's girl-friend, brought their baby to court. That poor baby had been born with no arms or legs. I felt they were using the baby for sympathy. From what I had heard, Jerry had never been there for Nicole or the baby. I did feel sorry for Nicole and hoped she would have the common sense to move on with her life and find some happiness. I hoped her family would be there to support her. For Galione's girl-friend, Janine, I wished misery. I knew she would not stick around and wait for her man. She was too selfish.

I was not prepared for the friends and family of the defendants to be given the opportunity to speak. It was sheer torture sitting there listening to how wonderful these two young men were. Galione presented the judge with seventy letters of support. Galione's parents enlisted their friends to speak on their son's behalf, saying, "He has always been so polite." I was going to be sick again. The judge even commented as to how disturbing it was to that so many of the letters claimed Galione was innocent. The parade of aunts, uncles, brothers, sisters, and teachers seemed to go on forever.

When it was finally my turn to speak, I walked to the front of the courtroom and faced the judge. I got through my letter. Tears stung in my eyes, but I fought them off. I did the best I could. When I finished, Mel Kardos asked permission to question me. That had not happened to anybody else all day. I looked at Matt, and he shook his head yes. The judge granted the permission. I was shaking. He asked me where I worked. I was stunned. What was his point? I told the judge I was scared to say where I worked. I did not want any of them to know where I worked. I knew Kardos wanted me to say I worked at *The Bucks County Courier Times*. He was going to say I had some-thing to do with the press coverage of this case. I was lucky if I got a pen in that building, let alone the power to drive the news. I turned to Kardos, smiled sarcastically, and answered I worked for a com-pany called GPN. He was clearly annoyed that he did not get the answer he wanted. It was the truth. GPN was Greater Philadelphia Newspapers. I did not lie. That's what was on my paychecks.

I nervously looked over at Laurie Mason; she was the writer for *The Bucks County Courier Times* who covered all trials and court-related events. She even had her own office in the basement of the courthouse. She smiled. I ran up to her as soon as it was over and asked her if I'd lied. She laughed and said no. She said it was amazing that I came up with the perfect truthful answer.

I found out later from the prosecutor and the reporters that they had *never, ever,* heard someone questioned after giving an impact statement. It was another excuse to hate Mel Kardos. What an arrogant man he was.

Judge Heckler gave a small speech. He said there had been many lulls in the fighting that night, and he said Jimmy and Jerry should have stopped.

Jerry Reeves asked to speak. He stood up and said he was not responsible for David's death. He said the real killer was still free. Peter Hall asked the judge to delay the sentencing so he could do more investigating. He was a moron; more investigating was not needed. More arrests were needed. Thank God the judge refused.

After all the fanfare, Judge Heckler sentenced Jimmy Galione to five to ten years in the state penitentiary for conspiracy to commit third-degree murder and a list of other charges. Jerry Reeves was sentenced to eight to sixteen years in the state penitentiary for third-degree murder and other charges.

My family just gasped. They were going to prison but for only five and eight years!

The moans and crying from their families was over dramatic and very annoying. How dare they? I remember Angela Galione screaming, "Why are they doing this to him?" I really wanted to punch her in her stupid face. Was she really that stupid? Why could she not see her brother for the murderer he was?

Jerry Reeves's little brother was crying, "Oh, Jerry." I did feel sorry for him; he was just a little kid. I hoped he would learn from this and not follow in his brother's shoes. I hoped his family would teach him right from wrong.

My first question for the court advocates was how long they would actually spend in prison. They said we would talk about it later.

I was in shock. What was Judge Heckler thinking? Five years, eight years, *for murder!* I felt like he was slapping the jury that had worked so hard in the face. Is that all he felt Dave's life was worth? I was so hurt. I felt so let down by him. I had admired him through this whole process. I felt he ignored the jury's findings and went with his own. This was a murder verdict. Did he think David deserved this? Was it possible he believed David started the fight? Did he not hear the testimony? David was just driving home. Galione and Reeves were out looking for someone to "mess up" that night. David, Joey, and Anthony did everything they could do to avoid the first fight, and then they were ambushed and ran for their lives when the second altercation began. If Heckler felt this was a mutual fight, he was wrong. He was very wrong. I was just so devastated.

The only good thing that happened that day was getting to see them led off again in handcuffs and shackles. They had to listen to *their* families and the pain they had caused them. I doubted they gave my family or David one thought. I doubted they even grasped the idea of how much damage they had done. Did they even realize they were going to hell? They were probably both just feeling sorry for themselves. I hoped they were scared to death about where they were headed. I hoped they feared for their lives.

Our court advocates told us we would be given the opportunity to try to keep them in prison for the maximum amount of time, which was the second number in the sentence. They also told us there would most likely be appeals filed. I wasn't paying attention; I wanted to get out of there.

I tried to wonder how David would have felt about the sentences. He probably would have been hurt but would have told us to move on. That was going to be difficult.

Jerry Reeves's mother was complaining that the trial was not fair. She was claiming her son was a scapegoat. She also complained about the racial makeup of the jury.

Had she forgotten her son confessed to hitting David in the head with the level? Did they have any guilt that they had not done *something* about their son's anger problem? Of course they didn't feel guilty, because poor Jerry was just being picked on by everyone.

Both of the defendants were being transferred to Bucks County Prison for ten days. They would then be transferred to state prisons to serve their sentences. Hopefully, they would be sent to a prison far, far away from my family. The farther away from us, the better. The thought of them being hauled far away gave me slight pleasure. The two families with no compassion would have to drive very far to visit their murderous children.

I hoped all the horror stories you hear about prison would happen to them. I hoped they would be beaten up and their existence in there would be unending misery. I hoped David's voice would come to them every night in their sleep, begging them not to kill him, calling out his son's name. I hoped the food would be crappy.

The Galiones were still whining that their son was innocent. I guess they forgot about the confession also. I guess they did not hear the same evidence we heard. I guess they forgot they had thrown him out of their house because of his drinking. I guess they forgot he was thrown out of college. I guess they just didn't want to face the truth. How about the fact they lied? Then there was the fact that they destroyed evidence. They should feel lucky they were not being charged. Their kid was a killer, and that was a fact.

How did Judge Heckler come up with these sentences? Why? They were not even close to the state sentencing guidelines he himself helped create while in the legislature. Was there anything we could do? Who did he think he was? Was he inexperienced? I needed answers, and I would get them.

Judge Heckler was a graduate of Central Bucks High School. He earned his bachelor's degree in political science at Yale and then his law degree from the University of Virginia. He was a prosecutor from 1972 to 1979, working up to rank of deputy. He also taught criminal justice at Bucks County Community College. In 1986, he became a state representative and was a state senator from 1993 until 1997. While in the legislature, Heckler helped craft the state of Pennsylvania's sentencing guidelines. He had just been a judge since 1998. I wondered if this was the first murder case for him since becoming a judge.

# For Court-Committed State Prison Population
## Minimum/Maximum Sentences (in years)
## Pennsylvania, 1993–2001

|  | '93 | '94 | '95 | '96 | '97 | '98 | '99 | '00 | '01 |
|---|---|---|---|---|---|---|---|---|---|
|  |  |  |  |  |  |  | (Dave killed) | (Trial) |  |
| Murder, 1st Degree | Life/ Death | Life/ Death | Life/ Death | Life/ Death | Life/ Death | Life/ Death | Life/ Death | Life/ Death | Life/ Death |
| Murder, 2nd Degree | Life/ Death | Life/ Death | Life/ Death | Life/ Death | Life/ Death | Life | Life | Life | Life |
| Murder, 3rd Degree | 10.2/ 22.8 | 10.3/ 22.9 | 10.4/ 22.9 | 11.1/ 23.1 | 11.4/ 23.6 | 12.1/ 24.2 | 12.3/ 25.7 | 12.9/ 25.7 | 13.7/ 28.6 |
| Murder, Unspecified | 13.2/ 19.5 | 9.4/ 20.1 | 9.6/ 20.8 | 11.5/ 22.6 | 10.3/ 22 | 9.3/ 20.2 | 9.9/ 21.8 | 10.7/ 21.8 | 11.4/ 24.6 |
| Voluntary Manslaughter | 5.6/ 12.0 | 5.7/ 12.0 | 5.8/ 12.3 | 5.9/ 12.6 | 5.9/ 12.6 | 6.0/ 13.1 | 6.3/ 14.0 | 6.8/ 14.0 | 7.2/ 16.0 |
| Involuntary Manslaughter | 3.4/ 7.9 | 4.1/ 9.1 | 4.1/ 9.1 | 3.9/ 9.0 | 4.0/ 9.6 | 4.0/ 9.7 | 4.2/ 10.3 | 4.5/ 10.3 | 4.8/ 11.8 |
| Homicide by Vehicle | 3.5/ 7.5 | 4.0/ 7.4 | 3.5/ 7.7 | 3.5/ 7.8 | 3.6/ 8.0 | 3.5/ 7.8 | 3.8/ 8.6 | 4.1/ 8.6 | 4.2/ 9.6 |
| Aggravated Assault | 6.2/ 13.6 | 6.3/ 13.6 | 6.1/ 13.3 | 5.7/ 13.4 | 5.8/ 13.8 | 5.9/ 13.8 | 6.5/ 14.7 | 6.3/ 14.7 | 6.3/ 14.8 |

Source: 2002 Fact Sheet, Pennsylvania Department of Corrections

When I saw this chart, I was astonished. These guys were convicted by the jury of third-degree murder. Although Galione was convicted of conspiracy to commit murder in the third, by law, it carries the same weight. The only logical thought I could come up with was that Judge Heckler disregarded the jury's ruling and chose his own. He wrote the guidelines. I felt so deceived. The minimum sentence in 2000 for third-degree murder was twelve point nine years. Reeves received eight years and Galion, five. The average maximum sentence for third-degree murder in 2000 was twenty-five point seven years. Reeves's maximum was sixteen years, and Galione's was ten years. From the best I could figure, Judge Heckler reduced the jury's rulings to voluntary and involuntary manslaughter. How dare he? I really wanted to know why he felt he had the arrogance to make this change. The jury had deliberated for fifteen hours. They gave up their time. They gave up their personal lives and worked for the citizens of Bucks County. They took their jobs seriously. They got it right. The conviction was murder, not manslaughter or assault.

People said to me, "Just be happy they were convicted." I would never forgive this man that I'd previously held in such high regard. I will never understand how he could sleep knowing he took it upon himself to devalue David's life. Whatever he was thinking, he was very wrong. I wished the worst karma on him and his family. I wished him embarrassment. I wished him pure *hell!*

Matt just kept saying we should be satisfied with the conviction. He too was confused by the sentence but told us to be satisfied for now. It was time for more arrests. That's what I told him. I had waited long enough; it was time.

I had no other choice but to use every resource available to make sure they served their maximum sentences. We had the right to register with the prison system and be able to track their every move. I vowed to be watching.

I signed up with the Pennsylvania Office of the Victim Advocate. I signed up to the Pennsylvania Corrections Center's website. I wrote to the attorney general of the state of Pennsylvania, hoping he could force Diane Gibbons to do her job, force her to make more arrests. I never got a reply.

I most certainly was going to be a more aggressive voter from this point on. There seemed to be *no* elected officials interested in working for the people. I would never again place a vote for *anyone* I had not fully investigated. I promised myself I would open my mouth about it too; I would share the information, whether good or bad, with anyone that would listen.

# Excerpt from Victim Impact Statement,
## submitted March 17, 2000, by Doreen M. Brinkerhoff

My name is Doreen. I am David's older sister. The oldest of five. I was fourteen when David was born. I could go on for hours talking about my memories of Dave and how much I loved him, but I won't. I am here to talk about how David's death has impacted me. I miss my brother every minute of every day. He did not deserve to be so brutally murdered. Birna did nothing to have her life so brutally changed. She is a really good kid. The way she is being treated now makes me really angry. She is being harassed. Friends and members of the Galione family have decided she has not suffered enough. This is the mentality Jimmy Galione was raised with. We did not hear at the trial how his family had thrown him out of the house because of his drinking problem, a problem he has had for years. Jimmy Galione and Jerry Reeves had a choice on April 24th, and they made the wrong one. They caused all this pain for their families and friends as well as ours. They made the wrong choice, and now they have to pay the price. Your Honor, I just want you to know that I have the utmost respect for you and the way you handled this trial. I am now asking you to please impose a sentence that is deserving of this brutal crime and one that will hopefully send a message to the young people in Bucks County that violence on our streets will not be tolerated.

# MORE ARRESTS, PLEASE?

A year had passed. We met at the memorial site on Wilson Avenue. Many of Dave's friends joined us there. Strangers stopped by to offer comfort. We lit candles and shared memories of Dave. Marina sang a beautiful song. We cried and hugged each other. The pain was still as real as it was a year before. Not enough time had passed. I still hated time. I was a year older; we all were. One thing I knew for sure was that on that night one year ago, my life changed forever. I was not the same person I was and would never be that person again. I was the big sister last year, a role I was proud of and enjoyed. I no longer wanted to be the big sister. I still had two younger brothers and a younger sister. I was detaching from them. I was doing the same with my own kids. I pretended I cared, but at that point, I was just too broken to do anything for anyone. I was terrified of losing another sibling. I was constantly terrified of losing one of my children or grandchildren. The fear would not leave. I thought the less

I knew about them at that time, the better. If I knew nothing, there was nothing to cause me fear.

I finally joined the NOVA homicide survivors group. They met once a week. I invited everyone in my family to join me, but I guess they were not ready, or perhaps they were in denial that they needed help at all. Every crazy feeling I had was validated that night. I was no longer alone in my nightmare. There were others. There were people there that had lost sons, daughters, parents, siblings, and friends to violence. As awful as everyone's story was, it was such a comfort that I was not alone in my pain. I also quickly realized it was going to be an extremely painful process. I cried the entire night after that first meeting.

When I still could not stop crying the next morning, I decided to visit my doctor again. I hated giving in to the need for medication, but my doctor convinced me I needed to give my body a break. I did not think the medication was helping me; I still felt pain and still had nightmares. The people I worked with told me they noticed a difference in me. They said I seemed to be concentrating a bit more on work and I was talking more. I hadn't realized I wasn't talking. I went faithfully to that group every Monday night for a year. The counselors from NOVA were amazing, to say the least, and were always there for me.

Jerry Reeves and Jimmy Galione were appealing to Judge Heckler. They claimed there was new evidence in the case. Matt told us there would be a hearing. He was not telling us what the supposed new evidence was. My kids had heard rumors that Mike Good had been at a party in Philadelphia, and some girl who happened to be from Bristol was saying she overheard him bragging and demonstrating how he repeatedly stomped on David's head. At first I was thrilled. Finally, at least Mike Good would be arrested. Those hopes were quickly dashed as Matt explained there was a possibility Galione and Reeves could have their sentences reduced if it were proven they were not the only ones guilty of killing Dave.

There was no medication in the world that could have stopped my anguish at this news. The justice system is so confusing. We know others were involved. We *know* Mike Good supposedly bragged about stomping on David's head. We also knew David had three fatal injuries—one caused by a hammer, one by the level, and one by blunt force. Was that blunt force caused by Mike Good's boots? This did not make anyone there that night less culpable. They were all guilty. I wanted them all arrested and in jail. I was tired of all the excuses. I was angry with the police. I was furious with the district attorney. I was tired of hearing about who said and did what and what evidence was old and what was new. I just wanted these idiots to get it together and arrest everyone who touched David that night.

The judge agreed to a hearing to have the new evidence presented. We had to stand in the hallway outside the courtroom. There was another proceeding going on. The Galione family was there. Every one of them showed up. They looked as if they had won some kind of a battle. They actually believed this new evidence was going to free their golden boy. It is still beyond me how they had no shred of remorse or compassion. I also saw Jerry Reeves's family in the hall. I had no real animosity against them except for the attempt to use Jerry's race as an excuse. They had at *least* offered us condolences for our loss. They too looked victorious, as if they had already won the battle. It was a small hallway toward the side of the courthouse. It was not the large, round hallway we were used to, the one where we could separate ourselves from the *enemy* family. In this hall, we were in close proximity. It was suffocating. Bonnie Reeves, Jerry's mother, was standing very close to me. With a huge smile on her face, she looked at me and asked if they had brought the boys in yet. I felt sick. She acted like a giddy teenager waiting to get a glimpse of a couple of rock stars.

The hearing was very brief. A young woman was put on the stand and told the judge her recollection of being at a party in Philadelphia. She said she walked into the kitchen and saw a person, a person she recognized as Mike Good, describing and demonstrating how he kicked and stomped David repeatedly on the head.

The defense attorneys immediately argued for the release of their clients due to this new evidence. I glared at Judge Heckler and was panicked. There was no way he would even consider releasing them, right? We would all have to wait. The judge was not making a decision that day. I would have loved to see Good arrested right there and led off in handcuffs to jail. I believed the girl's story. I believed Good had been bragging, and I definitely believed he stomped on David's head—many times.

A few weeks before this hearing or any news of the hearing, I had a dream. I was sleeping, and I opened my eyes and looked up at my ceiling. David was sitting on a swing that was hanging from my ceiling. I asked him who the *actual* killers were. He answered that it was Reeves and Galione and it was good. I started screaming at him. *What do you mean it was good? None of this is good. It is so bad; please stay with me. I want to talk to you.* With that, he was gone. It wasn't until the next morning that I put the name Good together. Was I dreaming, or had I finally seen the ghost I had desperately been waiting to see? It was just odd that shortly after that night, we were told of the witness and the hearing. Dream or not, I was convinced Mike Good was as guilty as the other two.

/////

I left that hearing that day trying to think positively. They just had to arrest Mike Good now. I waited anxiously. After several weeks and no arrest, I was told by Randy that it was up to the district attorney. They assured me they wanted to make the arrest and were ready to do so. I decided to give Diane Gibbons a call. I was unable to reach her, so I left a message. I waited two and then three days—no return call. I left another message. After several weeks, I shared my frustration at work. The publisher of the newspaper I worked for decided to place a call to her. I was shocked and very appreciative. He was told she was exhausted and not taking any phone calls. The editorial board jumped right on that and wrote a negative piece on our *tired* district attorney. I still did not get a call back. I continued to place calls to her office once a week and left messages. I was beginning to believe the rumors about her. I heard she was sleeping with the Bucks County lead investigator. I heard she was impossible to work with in the DA's office, and her assistant DAs shared their stories with me about what an egomaniac she was. They believed she didn't want to file more charges in this case because they would have to be murder charges, and she was not going to take any chance of ruining her 100 percent conviction rate.

I believed it was because that particular case happened in Bristol, the lower part of Bucks County, the heavily democratic portion of the county. There were no votes for her there. I honestly believed she felt it was a waste to her career. I believed she was a waste.

Diane Gibbons was a Bucks County prosecutor for twenty years before taking over the district attorney's job when Allen Rubenstein was elected judge. As a prosecutor, she'd tried sixteen murder cases with a 100 percent conviction percentage. She was the former chief of the child abuse unit, and her resume and election advertising called her an advocate for victim's rights. She most certainly was not advocating for us. Finally, after seven months of calling, I got a call from Randy, the police detective, telling me she would like to meet with me. I was thrilled, although still quite perturbed, at her arrogance.

When I sat down at that meeting, I got the distinct impression she did not want to be there. She seemed annoyed. Randy was there, the police chief was there, and a NOVA court advocate was there with me. She looked me straight in the eye and said she did not want to sign the arrest warrants because the police did not have enough evidence. Randy and the police chief argued with her. They felt they had the evidence.

She also wanted to wait until the Galione and Reeves situation was settled, because they had both filed appeals. Then she said she was in the middle of an election. I could not believe she said that. I told her I could not believe because of an election she would allow murderers to walk the streets. I was furious. Then it dawned on me. I had been right. She was a republican in the middle of a *tough* election. The murder happened in the lower part of the county, the democratic end of town. She was nothing but a politician. She would rather keep the murderers off the streets of the upper county, the republican part of the county. When I continued to badger her, she asked me if I realized that everybody involved that night would have to be arrested, including Joey and Anthony. She made it sound like a threat. I told her I did not care if she arrested Joey and Anthony. They had nothing to hide and had done nothing wrong. She did not like that answer. I wanted to reach across the table and choke her. I did believe that Randy and the chief wanted the other arrests. I believed it because they really argued with her. She would not budge. She did relent to looking into the evidence further. I did not believe she had any intention of looking into anything further. I had no other choice but to wait again.

Shortly after that meeting, the police chief, Frank Peranteau, was elected district justice in Bristol. A new police chief had to be chosen. My family gathered at the municipal building where the announcement was going to be made. We were told it was going to be Randy Morris, the detective, and we were thrilled for him. The decision had been made, and the meeting was just a formality. We liked him and believed he would fight harder for us as chief. My sister spoke on his behalf at the meeting.

Arnold Porter was the other choice. He too was a great police officer. I will never forget my friend Sam the policeman calling him Atom Ant. "He is a little guy but very tough," Sam would say. We did not know what his priorities would be as far as following the case through. When Porter got the job, I was disappointed. Politics worked against us again.

I liked Porter and wished him well. He was a good man. I was just so darn disappointed. I could only hope I was wrong and he would follow through with more arrests.

As I figured, it seemed Chief Porter was not interested in making the case a priority. I prayed he would have just a little mercy on us and try *something*.

I tried so hard to keep my hope alive. My frustration was pure anguish. Why wouldn't someone step up and do *something?*

I could not blame the media, any of them. They did their best to keep the story alive for as long as they possibly could. For their persistence, I will always be grateful to them, especially J.D. Mullane. J.D. kept the story in the news and continually questioned the district attorney and sentences. He continued to not only keep in contact with the police, but he kept in contact with my family. I had always been a fan of his writing, and I became a fan of the person.

# TRAGEDY STRIKES AGAIN

Another summer came and went. Another birthday came and went for David. He would have been twenty-eight. We gathered once again at the memorial. I was having trouble imagining David older. To me, I guess he would always be twenty-six. I heard somewhere that everyone in heaven is twenty-six. When you think about it, it does seem like the perfect age. I always had been afraid of dying. I wasn't afraid anymore. Wherever you go when you die, I knew someone there. I wasn't ready to go, not yet. I had so much I wanted to do here. I say that, but I really had no idea what I wanted to do.

I was continuing with my counseling faithfully. If I could offer one piece of advice to anyone that had a major trauma in their life, it would be to seek out and find someone or some group of people who had suffered the same trauma. It is hard work but well worth the pain. The validation alone was worth it for me.

I offered to do a project for NOVA. They had their yearly fundraiser in October. I put together an insert for the newspaper. It was like a small magazine. NOVA had been given a tract of land in the county park, Core Creek. I thought the project would raise awareness of the organization and all the great work they do and also raise funds for the planned arbor and gazebo for the park. The insert was smaller than I had hoped; I did not get much support from the paper, but I was proud of the piece. I learned a lot about the organization.

NOVA began in a church basement, as Women Organized against Rape. Over the next twenty-eight years, the agency grew to become a full-service victim organization known as The Network of Victim Assistance. They provided assistance to anyone who was the victim of a serious crime. They offered counseling, legal advocacy, education programs, and operated a hotline. All of NOVA's services are offered free of charge, regardless of income. They depended on very limited government assistance, community donations, and volunteers.

I had been taking anti-depressants for months now. I did not feel any different. People told me I seemed more like my old self and less sad. That was just outside though; inside, I was still full of sadness. The holidays would be coming again. The thought of Thanksgiving and Christmas was just so overwhelming. I was always a Christmas person. I loved baking, finding the perfect gifts, and just spending time with the family. I wanted that feeling back.

My relationship with my boyfriend was deteriorating. I knew it was an unhealthy relationship. He had left me just prior to David's death and then magically reappeared after the death. I began to realize he was using my grief and sadness as a way to control me. I never saw or even talked to my friends and barely saw my family. I seemed to go to work and go home—except on Mondays when I went to counseling. I really did not want to be around people other than those in my group. They knew how I felt. I knew, though, that I did need to start living again. I knew I had to make plans to end this relationship. In my grief, I had become so dependent on him. I knew that was not me. I had always been so independent. I knew it would not be easy, but I needed to wrap myself around the idea. I needed to move on.

When the phone rang at eleven o'clock one night, I panicked. I immediately got that, *uh oh, something's terribly wrong* feeling in my stomach. A very close family member had been carjacked and raped. I will not name her to protect her. I found myself in the emergency room again. It was Frankford Hospital again but this time at the new Bucks County location. I immediately wondered if one of David's attackers was responsible. Were they trying to send us a message to back off on our attempts for more arrests? How could such a tragedy be happening to my family again? This only happens in the movies, right? Were we such awful people that we deserved this, or was this normal, and all families went through stuff like this?

I really thought I would lose my mind for good that night. I was going into a sad, dark place, and I was afraid I would never come back. I could not catch my breath, and I could not think clearly. I just looked at the faces of my family, my kids in that emergency room, and my heart was broken. Why could I not protect them from this violence? Why were they being put through this horror at this young time in their lives? I tried to pull myself together for them, but I could not do it. I really tried hard to be in control. I just could not get it together. I wanted to crawl into that black hole and never come out.

I became afraid of everything. The dark was terrifying. Going to a store was just awful. If someone walked up behind me, I would panic. I would actually stop breathing. The problem was making my job so awful. I have no idea how I pulled it off. I was always sick I had six sinus infections in six months. The pain was unbearable, but it always made me think of the pain David went through, and I felt guilty. I went back to see my doctor. She changed my medication.

The holidays came, and I tried to be happy. I remember being at Joan and Dominic's house. Frank and Cheryl were sitting on the sofa with little Alexis. They made such a beautiful family. I was so happy they'd found each other. But that look was in Frank's eyes. I knew that look. That deep, endless sadness was in there.

Baby Julia was sitting on my son's lap, playing with wrapping paper. I was proud of my son. He was such a good daddy. I smiled at her, and she smiled back. Would I always look at her and remember she was born on the last day of the trial? She had no clue that she was born exactly nine months to the day of the night Dave was attacked. They say for every one God takes away, one is born. She was an angel. I had no doubt.

## /////

National Crime Victims Week was held in April. NOVA wanted to hold an ecumenical service in the brand new Victims Memorial arbor and gazebo in Core Creek Park. I was proud of the project I worked on for NOVA to bring awareness to the county of this special area and how important it was for victims and their families.

David's friends had raised the money to plant a tree in the arbor for David. The tree would be dedicated at the service. NOVA asked me to write and read a poem for the event. I do not know how I got through the reading, but I did. I was once again reminded we were not alone in our sorrow. Many other victims and survivors attended the moving service. Many of them I knew from my counseling group.

The service was held the same week of the second anniversary of David's death. Two years had gone by. When would there ever be more arrests? The only negative to the service was the fact that Diane Gibbons was there. I had to listen to her pretend she supported all victims. I lost all respect for her, not that I had much for her to begin with. There were just too many rumors about how fake she was. Why couldn't the police make her do her job? Why couldn't we make her do her job? I was beginning to realize that politics was just a game. These people make promises, get elected, and forget about the people that got them elected. They quickly forget they are supposed to work for the people, not for their career. That's why they call it public service. I just hated her. I honestly tried not to, but I did.

The carjackers and rapists were caught and brought to justice. They pleaded guilty to the charges, so there was no need for a trial. Thank God. One of them received fifteen years and the other thirty. They had been convicted of other crimes as well, so they would both be in jail for many, many years. I wondered if their beautiful, young victim would ever get past the horror of that night. It did not seem likely. She was resisting help and numbing herself with alcohol. I prayed so hard for her. As hard as I tried, I could not force her to get the help she desperately needed. I watched her break down, little by little, and then make one bad decision after another. I felt so helpless and, worse yet, hopeless for her, and it was breaking my heart. I tried everything I could think of to help. The situation became so desperate, I had no choice but to put her in God's hands and have faith.

Those two rapists took away her innocence that night, along with her hope. I hoped they rotted in hell. At least the judge that sentenced them was realistic with the sentences he handed down.

I continued to battle with depression. I was also constantly feeling sick to my stomach, had chronic sinus and ear infections, terrible nightmares, and debilitating panic attacks. I was always tired. I learned that grief can make you sick. I also learned that the rape of our family member, on top of David's murder, could cause something called post-traumatic stress disorder. The human mind can only process so much trauma at one time. My mind was certainly on trauma overload.

I started to think, *Who are we, the Kennedys?* I thought about that family. They had it all. They had money, power, and yes, more than their share of illness, trauma, and sorrow. They even had a few of their own criminals. How did they deal with their grief? Some, I guess, dealt well, and others not so well. Some went on to achieve greatness, and others went to jail. I wondered if they managed to stay close to one another through it all. Or, like me, did they feel disconnected from a once close-knit family? I wanted to be in a strong family. I wanted our family to work together and fight side by side for justice for David. It all sounded good, but my family was fractured. I was just waiting for the next shoe to drop.

That was my reality. When would the next tragedy strike, and when it did, would that be the end of my family for sure? Would we all be committed to some asylum?

I had issues with my mother, to say the least. The issues went back, of course, to that time when I was just thirteen and felt like she blamed me because her husband assaulted me. I entered into a business issue with her, and she ripped me off. I took her to court and won a judgment. She never paid. There were so many personal issues involved with making her pay, so I just decided to put it also in God's hands.

Imagine having to sue your own mother. She was lost to me. I would never, *ever* forgive her. I finally got past hating her, and she was just a ghost to me. To deal with *that* trauma, I saw another counselor. She told me I was wasting my time wanting my mother to be the picture of a mother I had in my mind. She never would be that person. She taught me if I didn't expect anything from her, I could not be disappointed when I received nothing.

I felt the need for my father in my life. I was not going to give up on him. I loved my stepmother, Janice. I also liked her. With them living in Florida, it wasn't always easy, but I wanted to always keep the lines of communication open.

My brother Nick was getting married to Gina. I was not happy with that idea. I had overheard Gina saying something mean to Nick's daughter, Alyssa, who was just a small child. I had no idea how to deal with that.

I was informed by Gina's mother that, at their wedding, I was to be seated next to Nick's father, the same man that sexually assaulted me when I was thirteen. I could not stand to be in the same room with him *ever.* I explained to her why I could not sit there. She made me feel like I was being ridiculous and making her life difficult. I could not bring myself to go to the wedding. I cried the whole day. I wanted my brother. I wanted to be happy for him and for him to be happy. I just could not face that man. What was worse, I never wanted my brother to know what his father had done to me.

I was having a hard time at work too. After months with no boss, I finally got one. This should have made my job easier, but he was horrible. Steve Hawkins was inexperienced, mean, and very bossy. I wanted coworker Rick Moretti to get the position. For months, I had been working in specialty advertising alone and, through some miracle, doing well at doing the job of three, along with everything else I was going through in my personal life. What a jerk Hawkins was.

I decided to go back to school. I needed to expand my choices. Just when I did not think I could take that stupid boss, Steve, another minute, I got a new partner. She was young and smart, and I liked her immediately. We had lunch together every day and became good friends. We were able to tag team the boss. I knew Steve was insecure. He knew I had done *his* job, and I had done it well. I tried to tell him I had no interest in taking his job, but that did not work; he was still a jerk. His boss, Tim Birch, was an even bigger jerk.

One day, a new customer of mine came into the lobby of the paper. She had started a new business and wanted to advertise. She had her daughter with her. While the customer filled out paperwork, I took the little girl to our break area. I bought her a candy bar from the vending machine and showed her around the building.

When I got back to my desk and was entering the customer information into the computer, I noticed an e-mail from Steve. It read: *Please refrain from bringing your children to work with you.* I saw red. I went right into Steve's office and told him it was not my kid. He knew it was not my kid. He knew my kids were grown-ups and my grandchildren were babies. His answer was to tell me Tim had made him send the e-mail. Tim wanted the message documented. I went into Tim's office and explained it was a customer. He shrugged me off, and that started a war. I never felt comfortable in that building again. It was a terrible feeling, because I loved my job. From that day on, I physically could not breathe in that building.

It was still so hard to pretend I was not sad every minute of every day. I was hypersensitive to any noise. I wanted to run as fast as I could from any situation that was not calm. Was I crazy? I felt crazy. I was scared. I wanted to feel normal. I wanted to be the person I was on April 24, two years ago. Would I ever be that person again? It was doubtful. I had to accept the fact that I was just a woman who had lost a brother tragically, just another face in the crowd with a story to tell. They say for every sad story you have, someone has one sadder. I believe that is true.

I find myself saying, "Well gee, so and so lost two brothers," or "This one lost a brother and a sister. I am so lucky I only lost one." It's bizarre when you think about it. Is there any way to measure loss? Do we just do this to make ourselves feel better?

I think the human psyche is so complicated no one could answer these questions. Our human brains only allow us to process trauma in pieces, sort of like the saying that God will never give you more than you can take. I hoped he was done trying me.

# IT'S ALL ABOUT ME

That summer, I was diagnosed with post-traumatic stress disorder. The only thing I knew about this disorder was that it was associated with soldiers. I was taking psychology courses, so I looked it up. I had all the symptoms: flashbacks, shame, guilt, feeling numb, anger, hopelessness, trouble sleeping, nightmares, trouble concentrating, easily startled and frightened, stomachaches, headaches, poor relationships, and not enjoying any activity that used to be fun.

I would lie awake in bed at night and recall all the tragic events in my life. I would then give each event a number. I would get so frustrated because, when I would start to think about a certain event, I would forget where I was numerically and have to start all over again. I knew this was obsessive -compulsive behavior. I didn't care.

My grandmother, my father's mother, died when I was very young. I really do not remember her, but I have always missed her.

My father was an only child, so she would have only had my sister, Dede, my brother Frank, and me for grandchildren. My mother's mother had thirteen.

When I was in second grade at Saint Christopher's Elementary School in North East Philadelphia, a boy put a worm in my orange drink. When nothing came through the straw, I lifted the straw, and there was the worm, just dangling there. I was terrified and am still terrified of worms to this day.

My parents divorced when I was in fifth grade. They did fight a lot. My dad was working second shift, and a creepy man used to come to our house when my dad was at work. I was naïve and really had no clue what was going on; I just knew it didn t feel right. My father was a good dad back then. He would play in the yard with us, and he took us on great vacations. He did have a bad temper, and he wanted things to be just so in the house, but overall, he was a fun dad. He had just about finished work on our attic, and it was going to be my very own room. He built a desk and shelves himself, and I was so excited to not have to share a room with my sister anymore. Then one day, my mother said we were moving. The next day, I was living in an apartment and going to a new school. I had trouble making friends at Saint John the Evangelist in Yardley. I was embarrassed that my dad did not live with us. Instead, there was a creepy guy living with us. The apartment was in a bad neighborhood in Morrisville. Our bus stop was right next to the public school bus stop. I was teased horribly by the public school kids. They would actually pull my hair and push me. When I told my mother, she said nothing. I would sit in the back courtyard after school and play with the little kids out there. One little boy, Michael, was so cute. His mom, Diane, was nice too, and I think she felt sorry for me, because she was always getting me stuff. Every couple of days after school, I would babysit Michael and his little sister, Michelle. I really became attached to Diane. She spent time with me, listened to me, and even went to the bus stop in the morning with me one day and seriously threatened the bullies. They never bothered me again.

I did not see my dad for a long time. I felt sorry for him. He was all alone with our dog, Waggles.

There we were in this crappy apartment, and my mother was going to have a baby. They say to be specific with your prayers. That lesson took me awhile to learn. The good thing was, my mother and Nick were shopping for a house. I was excited about that. I hated that apartment. The house was nice and in a nice neighborhood. It was called Valley Green and in Fairless Hills. I transferred to St. Francis Cabrini School, and I hated the school. I made friends in the neighborhood, so the school was bearable. I had confrontations with the nuns, and in eighth grade, I was confused with religion. I did not want to accept their minimal answers to my questions. I challenged them, and they did not like that. My mother was having a baby with a man she was not married to, was still married to my father, and she was having crazy séances in our house. It was embarrassing.

When I was eighteen, I found out that my mother had cashed in *my* life insurance policy to buy *that* house. She apparently won control of the policy in her divorce from my father. This was a policy my father had paid into ever since I was born; it was supposed to go toward my education, wedding, or whatever. It was not supposed to buy my mother and her creepy boyfriend a house.

When I left my childrens' father, all those years ago, had I ruined their lives? Those were just the crazy thoughts I gave numbers to as I tried to fall asleep at night. I also thought about all those premonitions I'd had about David. The guilt for that one was unbearable.

I was still in an awful relationship. After I counted all the horrible things I had done in my life and all the awful things that had happened to me, I would try to plan my escape. How could I do it with the least amount of confrontation and angst?

Yeah, it was pretty obvious I was a nut case. Now I had this traumatic stress thing too. I wasn't the only one suffering with this illness or disorder. Most of my family had the thing too. If someone slammed a door, I jumped out of my skin. If a car followed me too closely, I had to pull over. It was such a release to talk about these episodes in my homicide survivors group. I was also educating myself on the disorder and working on getting it under control. I did not want to be on medication for one minute longer than I had to be.

Toward the end of the summer, my symptoms started to lessen. Unfortunately, as my mental symptoms lessened, my physical ones seemed to be getting worse. I decided I needed to take better care of myself. I bought vitamins that were supposed to help with energy. I took vitamins C and E. I bought calcium supplements. They were like chocolate-caramel candy, so I enjoyed taking them. I became obsessive about washing my hands. Germs were the enemy. I was so tired of the sinus infections. Two weeks after starting my new health regime, I got sick to my stomach. I had pains in my sides. I took some Advil and went to bed. When I got up in the morning, I had a rash all over my body. My throat and chest felt like they were on fire. My face was swollen, and I had a fever. I was admitted to St. Mary's Hospital.

After six days on IV liquids and antibiotics, I finally got a diagnosis. The rash was caused by a *turtle virus*. I had recently bought my granddaughter Allyson a turtle and had helped her clean the cage. The virus had a very long name, but apparently, there was no cure for it other than antibiotics and cream for the rash. I would have it for life. It could remain dormant for years or become chronic.

*Great*, I thought, *now I am scared to death of turtles.*

The burning pain in my throat and stomach was caused by an allergic reaction to those calcium supplements I loved so much. They were made with shellfish, which I am *very* allergic to. My intestines had been burned so badly I was unable to eat for two weeks. Those Burger King commercials were killing me. I was starving. They also told me my appendix was slightly swollen and that I had diverticulitis. I remained in the hospital for another week. The whole experience was scary, but honestly, I was relieved that there was a *physical* cause and not a mental one.

By early September, I was feeling much better, mentally and physically. I tried to enjoy my job again and spent as much time as possible with the kids. My counseling was going really well, and

I actually felt like I was helping the newer members of the group. I continued my classes, because there was no doubt in my mind I wanted to help victims and survivors. I wanted to become a counselor.

Then it all came crashing down again—9/11 happened. I went in to the paper early that morning with plans of catching up on some work. A friend called and asked if I had heard a plane crashed into the World Trade Center. She knew I had a friend that worked in that building. My partner had arrived, so together we walked down to the newsroom, and there it was on all the televisions. When the second plane hit, we thought it was a re-play of the first. Having a father that worked in the airline business, I knew immediately it was not an accident. *No* pilot would crash into a building. There was too much water close by.

I went back to my little cubby office and then heard the pentagon had been hit. I was terrified. My partner and I went out back to smoke a cigarette and watched five military jets wiz by. Our building was located right on the Delaware River, and they were headed north—to New York, we imagined. I had to get out of that building. I decided I would try to salvage the day and visit some clients. Glenn Beck was on the radio in my car. Sometimes I listened to talk radio, other times music. That day was a news day. The more I listened, the sadder I felt. Every client I visited was glued to their televisions, just stunned. I called all of my kids; I just had a need to know they were safe. I went home and watched the news all night. It was just one horror story after another.

Of course, it was all about me. I had lost a brother to murder. I had an awful childhood, just a horrible life altogether, and then that happened. Now our whole country was being threatened by terrorists. All of my hard work in therapy was going down with those buildings. I wanted to crawl back into my dark hole. I felt sick again.

As I continued to watch through the night, all of a sudden, it wasn't about me anymore. I watched the faces of strangers not knowing whether their loved ones had survived. The thought of all those mothers, fathers, brothers, sisters, and friends that lost their loved ones that day was overwhelming. Would they end up like me, afraid of their own shadows and physically sick? I prayed for them, and I cried for them.

In November I was back in the hospital. I had terrible pains in my side. At St. Mary's Hospital, they said it was probably my diverticulitis acting up. After seven days of nothing but IVs and antibiotics, nothing was better. The pain was horrific. Morphine was doing nothing to help. Because I worked at a newspaper and handled mail, they thought I might have been exposed to anthrax. I fell asleep at one point and woke up with six doctors surrounding me dressed in what looked like space suits. Talk about scared. Well, the six of them could come up with nothing, so I was transferred to the University of Pennsylvania Hospital. There they said my appendix had burst and that I had an intestinal tear. There was also some kind of a tumor in my large intestine, and I was told it was probably cancerous. The nurses assured me that I was in good hands, because the doctor that would be operating on me was the best intestinal surgeon in the *world*. For some crazy reason, I wasn't scared, until I was on that operating table and saw that there were eight interns in there that would be *observing* my guts. The one had the job of drawing with a marker on my stomach. He noticed and mentioned my terrible stretch marks. How embarrassing that was. He told me he was studying to become a plastic surgeon and would be in charge of closing me up. He said he would throw in a little tummy tuck. That was the last thing I remembered before going under.

I woke up in recovery, confused yet alert enough to know something was wrong. People were running around and yelling, and I was out again.

When I came to again, I could see I was in a room, and I saw my kids. My first thought was, *I'm alive.* I quickly realized I was on a ventilator and could not move. I am so claustrophobic and thought I should have been freaking out, but I guess the drugs were good.

My kids looked scared. I hated putting them through this. My sister-in-law Cheryl commented to everyone that I looked good. I know she was trying to make everyone feel better. I did not believe her; I was sure I looked awful, but it did make me smile inside. I just lay there listening to everyone talk, only half comprehending. What I did comprehend was when the doctors came in and said a tumor they removed was not cancerous and that they had removed most of the diverticuli and, of course, my rotten appendix. They told me I would be just fine. I wanted to ask them if they had to give me one of those bag things; that was one of my biggest fears, but of course, I was unable to talk. They also explained to me what had happened in recovery. My blood pressure had bottomed out, and they thought they were going to lose me. That didn't really sink in because of the drugs.

There isn't much else to do when you can't move or talk, so I just thought. I thought about my Aunt Renee, who was amazing at doing horoscope charts. She had done mine years ago, and I remembered her telling me I would have serious health issues but would come through them fine. She also told me I would meet a man later in my life, fall in love, and marry him. She told me he would not be from around here. She told me his name would be John.

A few hours after the surgery, one of the interns told me my doctor's twenty-one-year-old daughter had just passed away from brain cancer. I felt so intensely sad for him. How heartbreaking it must be to be considered God (that's what the nurses called him) and to be unable to save your own child. I wondered if it was me causing all these bad things to happen.

Was it possible I was cursed? Was it because I went to see that psychic the night Dave was attacked? Whatever bad or evil spell was on me, I lay in that bed and vowed to remove it from my life. I vowed to *change* my life. I would be kind to everyone. I had had enough of the tragedy. I was going to do for my kids what I had promised myself back after Dave died. I was going to show them that good can come from evil. I was taking control, oh yeah, as soon as I could move and talk again. I started making lists of all the good things that had happened in my life. There would be no more *poor me*, bad-things-that-had-happened-in-my-life lists. I would no longer be a slave to negativity. I was going to get well, finish school, leave my awful relationship, and start a brand new life.

Then something wonderful happened. Joanie whispered in my ear that she was going to have a baby. Allyson was six, so I had almost given up on the idea of her having a sibling. I wanted to hug her, and I did have tears, but I still could not talk or move. What wonderful news, and what inspiration to get well and get home.

It was Thanksgiving morning when one of the interns came in and said it was time for me to breathe on my own. As quickly as he was saying it, he pulled the ventilator tube from my throat and tubes from my nose. My chest hurt badly. I was gasping for a breath. He told me to just relax and let my body do the work. In other words, don't try to breathe. He told me someone would be in later that evening to get me up out of bed.

*Holy crap,* I thought. *They really think I am getting up out of bed?*

They brought me some green Jell-O. I hate Jell-O, especially green. *Some Thanksgiving dinner,* I thought. I caught myself and said, "No negativity. I am alive. There will be other Thanksgivings." I tried not to be sad that there had been no one to see me all day. Ever since that time, Thanksgiving has been a very meaningful holiday for me. For all the horror in my life, I certainly had my share of blessings too. I never wanted to forget to be thankful.

Early in the evening, my sister walked in with a beautiful bunch of flowers. The nurses started filling the room with flowers that had arrived earlier in the week. They were not allowed to be in intensive care, so I was thrilled to have them and appreciated the nurses reading all the cards to me.

My sister left, and there was nothing to do but lie there and look at the big clock on the wall and the beautiful flowers. I looked at the clock because they had taped a button to my finger and told me to push the button every ten minutes. It was like playing a video game. The janitor came into the room, emptied the trash, and mopped the floor. I paid no attention to him; it was still difficult to talk. I guess he was watching me, and he said, "I heard tell if you push that button one second before the ten minutes, you can push it twice." Well that sounded like a challenging game, so I watched the second hand and got the two pushes on the first try—and the second and the third.

I was up on one of the top floors next to the helicopter pad. I didn't realize that. I saw bright blue lights and heard loud noises. I saw blue people walking past the window. They scared me, so I went back to my game. I thought I saw frogs jumping in my flowers and buzzed for the nurse with the button that was taped to my other finger. When she came in, I told her there were blue people trying to get into my room and frogs were loose all over. She said she saw nothing and left quickly.

*This is it,* I thought to myself. *I have gone crazy.* I was just going to pretend I was normal. I would close my eyes and convince myself there was nothing there. I opened my eyes, and there they were, hopping all over the flowers. What did they want?

My brother Frank walked into my room with Cheryl. I made them check everything. They said they saw nothing. The puzzled look on Frank's face would have made me laugh if I wasn't scared to death. They did not stay long.

I was awake most of the night, too scared to sleep. I was terrified the blue people were going to get me and take me somewhere. I had figured out they were aliens, and the spaceship was right outside my window. The frogs were their spies. I tried to concentrate on my game but kept missing the second hand because I was distracted by the frogs.

The sun finally came up, and a cleaning woman was watering the flowers and started to scream. It turned out there *were* critters hopping around, but they were crickets. They called a janitor to take care of them.

I was relieved that I had seen something jumping around. What about the blue people and the spaceship? Hmm … that was a mystery!

One of the interns came in and asked me about my night. He said I had every nurse on the floor scared to come into my room. I

told him I was just playing this game with the button and kept seeing things. He removed the morphine drip. That was the end of that
game. He gave me some Dilaudid, and I slept most of the day.

I woke up early in the evening and had some more awful green
Jell-O. A nurse came in and told me it was time to get up and go for
a walk. I got my feet onto the floor and slowly tried to stand. The
nurse said that was a good start and we would try again later.

Six days later, I was headed home. It was a long, tough recovery,
but I was determined to maintain my positive attitude.

## /////

I absolutely believe that grief can *cause* physical illness. There are studies being done. I hope they find something that can help people earlier
in their grief so they can avoid the physical side effects. I hope more
counselors will begin to stress the fact that *you must take care of you!*

Bad things happen to good people. That's just the way it works.
But life has to go on. You have to find someone or something to
focus on, starting with yourself. When you think about it, there are
so many great things that have been born of tragedy. For example,
Miles for Hope, born from the death of a brain cancer patient, and all
of the great programs for breast cancer were started because someone
that was loved died of the disease. Survivors of Suicide was started
out of the pain of one parent losing their child to suicide. NOVA was
started because one woman was raped and was *not* going to tolerate
being a victim for the rest of her life. I could go on and on: the March
of Dimes and the Red Cross, just to name a few more. Now it was
my turn. I had no idea what it would be but prayed God would lead
me to my answer. I would find a way to turn the horrific death of my
brother into something that could help somebody, somewhere.

It had been two years, and there were still no new arrests. In my
newly positive frame of mind, I decided to put this matter in God's
hands. I still checked in with the district attorney's office and the
police. I just refused to let it get me down.

The appeals process was moving along, and so far Galione's and Reeves's sentences remained the same. They were not giving up without a fight.

They still did not understand the impact of what they had done. They had no idea how *lucky* they were that Judge Heckler had given them the sentences they were given. I just kept my faith in God and my faith in our justice system. Whoever said the wheels of justice move slowly knew what they were talking about.

I decided I had had enough of my job. My partner quit, and without her it was unbearable. I wanted my own business again. I discussed it with my ex-partner, and together, we came up with the idea to start a gift basket company. It was the first step in my plan to get out of my mundane relationship. I had to keep my job until the business could support me, but it was a lot easier knowing the end was in sight.

# THE BABY PARADE

I was still recovering from my surgery, but I did join my family for Christmas Eve. I was still sad and missed David, but I vowed to maintain my positive mood. We talked about the new baby we would have with us next Christmas. Allyson was so excited. It felt good to have something to look forward too.

This new baby would have no idea what we had lost. This baby deserved to be born into a healthy family, a family that was together and strong.

In February, the business was starting to do well. I had an awful day at the paper and was still there at eight o'clock, waiting for ads to come in electronically. It had been snowing, and I was getting nervous about driving home. I sat at my desk, waiting and thinking. I was frustrated, so I started to pray.

*God,* I said, *please just get me out of this place. I will take whatever you give me; just get me out of here.* Another employee who was stuck there waiting walked up to me and said, "Go home. You look like you have had enough." He said he would take care of my ads when they finally arrived. I could not thank him enough.

I walked out of that building feeling so positive. I had asked God for a plan, and I knew it would come. I cleaned the snow off my car and headed home. As I rounded the on ramp and merged on to the highway, I glanced sideways for a moment and saw it coming.

I was stunned and sat there for a moment. I realized there was another car in my front seat. We were stuck there in the middle of a snowy highway. I panicked. Another car, without a doubt, would be hitting us from behind. My first thought was to get out. I could not feel my right leg or arm. I felt no pain at that moment. That is, until I saw the red lights pull up behind my car; then I felt the pain. My face was hurting. I had excruciating pain in my left leg and side. The man who was driving the car that hit mine was running around screaming. I had no idea what he was saying. A police officer was screaming, "Are you okay?" I could not roll my window down to answer, so I just shook my head no.

As the EMTs put me on the gurney and started toward the ambulance, they slipped and fell. Luckily, they had me strapped down, so I did not fall off. As they got their footing and continued toward the ambulance, I looked up to the sky, which I actually never saw. I just saw snow. I looked up there and said, "LORD, this is not what I had in mind." They took me to St. Mary's Hospital. They said I had a broken hip and that they were waiting for a surgeon to come in for surgery.

My daughter Joan arrived, and I told her to get me out of there. There was *no way* I was having surgery in that hospital. Well, the next thing I knew, they said they had made a mistake; my hip was not broken, and I could go home. I went home and went to bed.

When I woke in the morning, I was in excruciating pain. It turned out I *did* have a fracture in my hip and a fractured jaw. I decided against the hip surgery after a great deal of research. I was not going to allow any of these events get me down. I asked God for a way out, and I got one. The recovery took months.

On good days, I worked hard at the basket business. I was determined to not *ever* have to go back to work for the newspaper. I loved the newspaper and the people I worked with; it was just a couple of thorns running the place that made it impossible for me to be happy there.

In March, I got the news that my daughter, Jillian, was pregnant. She had only been with Kevin, her boyfriend, a short time, so of course I was worried. They assured me they were committed to one another and the baby, so my worries faded. I realized I would be having two grandchildren born six months apart. I felt excitement. I had not felt *happy* in so long that it was almost frightening.

Julia would soon be two. It had been two years since the trial ended. I had to find a way to stop associating her birthday with the end of the trial. She didn't deserve that. She was a beautiful baby. Kyle was growing, and we hoped he would soon be able to eat on his own without the feeding tube. Little Michael was growing up so fast. I had to force myself to see *Michael* when I looked at him and not see David. It just wasn't fair to have him miss something, a daddy that he would never know. We would all be there for him when he was older and had questions.

I was honestly disappointed in my brothers Frank and Nicky. I felt they were not stepping up for Michael. I just felt they should be spending time with that little boy and giving him everything they believed David would have wanted him to have. I was disappointed in my own son also. Birna was a single mom now, and like so many other single moms, she had to work, take care of and make a home for her son, and manage to keep the lights on at the same time. No one had the right to judge her for anything she did or did not do. It just wasn't fair to her when she was just trying to find a way to cope.

In April, I was asked to do another poem for NOVA's ecumenical service. I wanted my poem this year to be a little more positive, empowering.

There were so many people there that had lost loved ones on 9/11. My heart was breaking for them. Would they ever have justice? Would they ever have the answers they desperately needed?

It was also the third anniversary of David's death. Although I focused on staying positive, I allowed myself to miss him. I had an overwhelming desire to make him proud of me. I also wanted my kids to see me smile again.

When I would make a negative comment about the sentences or other arrests being made, there were actually people who would say to me, "When are you going to get over that?" I did not let these comments anger me. I had every right to feel sad when I was sad. I had every right to miss my brother. I had every right to be angry with a system that was more interested in good percentages and winning elections than it was about protecting people. I was just determined to take my anger and turn it into positive energy. Anger had been like a heavy bundle of bricks hung around my neck. It was so heavy that I could not accomplish anything. Do not get me wrong; I did not suddenly turn into little miss sunshine. I *was* still angry. I just did not let it control me.

On June 10, 2002, Dominic Angelo Nocito III was born. He struggled to breathe. He had some fluid in his lungs. After a few scary hours, he was fine. The nurses in the nursery at Lower Bucks Hospital assured me it was a common problem with babies born via C-section. He also developed jaundice. Joan had it, and so did Allyson. At least I knew what that was. It was still awful seeing the tiny little guy under those lights with his eyes covered.

When I finally was allowed to hold him for the first time, I was overcome with an empowering feeling of hope. My family had a future, and I was holding it in my arms.

Allyson was so excited to be a big sister. She was so protective and actually very bossy over who could hold her brother and when. It was adorable and annoying at the same time.

When a photographer I recognized from *The Bucks County Courier Times* showed up at the hospital nursery, I was surprised.

When I asked him why they were doing a story on our little one, he told me to do the math. It was nine months since 9/11. Apparently, many babies were expected to be born that week. The tragedy that struck our country brought people together. Everyone just wanted to love each other, to hold on to who and what they had. Yes, that baby boy's eyes gave me a lot of hope.

In September, I learned my son and his wife were expecting. I was ecstatic and honestly overwhelmed. I was having a grandchild every six months.

I sat on the front porch with Allyson and asked her, "Allyson, how did I ever get this lucky to be having so many babies coming into our family?"

She thought for a minute and then looked up at me and said, "Mom-Mom, Uncle David knows how much you love babies. He is just going to keep on sending them down from heaven so you don't have time to be sad anymore." I looked up at the sky, and just at that moment, there was a beautiful rainbow. I cried and smiled. How is it possible for a seven-year-old to know the exact thing to say to make me believe? She amazed me.

After a long night of labor and an emergency morning C-section, on December 17, 2002, Morgan Layla Timm was born. I was only able to see her for a moment as they were rushing her into the intensive care nursery. She looked so tiny. I noticed a small patch of strawberry blonde hair and chubby little cheeks. Because Jill developed a fever during labor, they had to make sure the baby did not have an infection.

Jill was released after five days, and I will never forget going onto the elevator with her to take her home. It hit both of us as the elevator door closed that we were going home without the baby. I will never forget the pain in my own baby girl's eyes that day. I wanted to fix it for her, but there was nothing I could do.

What a miracle my Jill has always been. Every day, I thank God for her. I prayed to Mary the blessed mother; I thanked her for my beautiful daughter and asked her to watch over Morgan and Jill.

After a very frightening seven days, Morgan came home to join our family on Christmas Eve. It would have been unbearable to celebrate Christmas without our little peach.

/////

I always dreaded the holidays without Dave. Time still had not taken away the pain. I could not help but imagine how happy he would be for Joan and Jill. I imagined him sitting on the floor, playing with his little boy and his nieces and nephews. I felt guilty for feeling happy. I thought about what Allyson said, and I smiled.

/////

Another new year, and still there were no new arrests. Julia was turning three. Three years since the trial ended. I had not heard anything from the police. I felt a sting of guilt. I was so busy enjoying my newest little angels that I had no idea where the case stood. The appeals process had to be finished by now. I would never give up. I gave Randy a call. He assured me he had not forgotten about David and was still actively working on the case. I believed him but felt defeated. Would it ever happen? I felt so powerless at times, but I would never give up the fight for justice.

Our country was at war. I became addicted to cable news. I did not sleep; I just kept watching. The reporters were imbedded with the troops, and I was imbedded with the reporters. Our troops were amazing. They just rolled into Iraq and took it over. I had fleeting thoughts that this could possibly be the best marketing campaign I had ever seen, but I did not want to believe in the possibility of deception. The rumors were running rampant. A lot of people *believed* that 9/11 was an inside job. It was all just so creepy and really messing with my positive attitude.

I was still in therapy and still in school. Depression was a daily battle that I vowed to win. The business was a struggle at times, but I did have a new baby to look forward to; overall, we were doing very well. I loved making the gift baskets and delivering them. It was a great feeling to have a job that always made people smile.

The ecumenical service in April was as moving as always. I did not do a poem or speak that year. I was a bit disappointed. There were new cases. There were new victims. It was their turn. Had it really been four years since we lost David?

I felt panic. Dave's case was old and cold. It was only being worked on when there was nothing else to work on. Was I wrong for wanting these other arrests? I did not feel wrong. Why were people telling me to be happy with what we got as far as sentences and move on with my life? Was I being selfish because I did not want Dave to be forgotten? I just wanted to scream!

In May, I was invited to join NOVA's board of directors. I was honored, to say the least. It sounded so important, but I had no idea how to be a board member. This agency had become such an important part of my life, and I owed them so much. I think David would have been proud. I would do whatever I could to make a difference. I wanted to help others whose lives were struck by violence.

My son's wife, Marlana, was having trouble with her pregnancy. She had been hospitalized several times with kidney stones. After a visit with her in the hospital, I decided to take Julia home with me. I had a strong intuition not to leave.

We walked in the door, and my phone rang. My son said, "Come back. The doctor is going to deliver the baby now." There was something going on with the baby's heart rate. I scooped Julia up, and back we went to the hospital.

As we walked down the hall, they were wheeling the baby out of the operating room. I was so scared. Was he okay? Was Marlana okay?

So on June 16, 2003, after yet another emergency C-section, James Dylan Brinkerhoff was born. I held him and thanked God he was healthy. My son looked so handsome holding his new baby boy. I was so proud of the daddy he was. Julia adored him. I still worried about the trauma he had in his life, but at that moment, he looked so happy, so at peace.

David would have been so happy for him. He would have teased him a little. I could just close my eyes and imagine the two of them going back and forth. I fought off the tears and forced a smile. It was a good day. I had just been blessed with new life three times, exactly six months apart. My three musketeers—who could ask for more? I hoped they would always be close.

My kids never had cousins their ages. I started having kids so young. My kids were old enough to babysit their cousins when they came along. It had been like that for Nicky and David too. We were all so much older. My kids were more like Nick and Dave's siblings or cousins.

My cousin Rob is six months older than I am and my cousin Jim is six months younger. We spent a lot of time together as kids. We were the three musketeers. I love when good history repeats itself.

When my boyfriend was giving me a hard time about spending time with the babies, I knew I had to move on. It was time for him to go. No one who loved me and knew what I had been through would deprive me of something that gave me such joy. He was also causing problems between my business partner and me. He did not understand my commitment to NOVA. He asked why I didn't put Dave behind me and get on with my life. He asked—no, he demanded—to know why I would want to be involved with other people's horror.

What he could not understand was that my commitment to NOVA had nothing to do with not wanting to move on past my own trauma. It had everything to do with moving on. I wanted to make a difference, to be with other people who cared. I wanted to *help* others. I knew I could not stop violence from happening, but I knew I could make a difference when it did happen. I was a bit ashamed of the fact that it took my own traumas to get me involved.

I had always been a person who cares deeply, but that was it, just a feeling of caring. I knew now that I never wanted anyone in Bucks County who lost a loved one to murder to feel alone. I never wanted them to face a courtroom without a NOVA legal advocate holding their hand.

The holidays were here again. This year it was chaotic. The three little musketeers were into everything. Dominic was walking and starting to talk. Morgan was crawling and still looked like a sweet little peach. Little Jimmy was the quietest, sweetest baby. Julia and Allyson were little friends, just adorable.

Michael was getting so big. He looked so much like Dave, it was painful every time I looked at him. I had to remind myself to not let him see my emotions. I did not want to feel sad when I looked at him. I was so thankful to God that he was here. He was just a little boy. I tried thinking of the day he was born every time I saw him. That was such a beautiful experience. Birna might disagree, after me getting her to the hospital so late. But it was working for me.

I was missing Heather and Kyle. I had not seen much of them. Kyle was getting bigger and stronger and doing well. Matt and Heather had bought their first house. Kyle would finally have some room to move around with his walker. Birna and I had a great time painting Kyle's room. I painted my first sky on his ceiling. Well, sort of. It resembled a sky. The room came out adorable.

Another new year came and went. Julia was now four. Four years since the trial, and no new arrests. I began to doubt it would ever happen. I did not know where else to turn for justice. I had to have faith and put it in God's hands.

Spring arrived. It was now five years since Dave had passed away. Saying *passed away* sounds so gentle and quiet. It sounds almost easy. You want to picture a meadow and soft music playing with angels carrying you up to heaven. That was not working for me. There was *nothing* gentle about David's death. It was horrific and painful. He died begging for his life and thinking of his son. I felt like I was the only one that cared that murderers walked the streets of Bristol. I could not make the police arrest them. I could not make the district attorney give a damn. I felt so helpless.

I had no choice but to put it in God's hands. Some people stop believing in God when tragedy strikes. I do not know why, but it never dawned on me to believe or not believe. I was far from being a religious person. I think *spiritual* is more what I always was. I know I prayed like I had never prayed in my life while David was fighting for his life. I certainly questioned why God would take this man from his wife and baby. I knew the answer to that one. God did not take him away; the *killers* took him away. It was their free will, and they made the wrong choice. For me, it was as simple—and yet as complex—as that.

Another year, and I was still in this hopeless relationship. This guy needed help, and I was not going to fix him. I always thought I could fix anything. I felt like my feet were stuck to the floor. What was holding me back?

The answer to that question was eye opening. I was still there because I did not want to lose anything else—the key word here being *thing*. I had a beautiful home. It was furnished and decorated exactly the way I wanted. I had the biggest dining room and could actually fit the whole family for meals. I had worked my butt off to get all this *stuff.* It became clear to me that the fight to keep what was *mine* would be more than I could handle physically or emotionally. If I wanted out, I was going to have to leave. I was going to have to leave all the *things* I loved and start all over again.

My kids hated the relationship. They knew I was being abused both physically and emotionally, and they were tired of me telling them I was going to leave. I had to find a way to get my feet unstuck from that floor.

My baby parade continued. In October, we found out Heather was expecting. I was scared for her. We all were. If anyone deserved a miracle, it was Heather. I had no doubt God chose the right parents for Kyle. I was in awe of the way she loved and protected that baby. Just imagine how scary it would be to deal with feeding tubes, gagging, and endless doctor visits, not to mention the constant fear of not knowing how long your child would live. Yet here she was, this amazing young woman making it all look so easy.

Joan was scared. I think she was more frightened than Heather and Matt were. Joan wanted more than anything for Heather to experience what it was like to have a healthy baby.

I will never forget the afternoon I was at Joan's house and Heather called. Joan answered the phone and just started crying. I panicked and started to cry. "The baby is one hundred percent healthy," she screamed. We both ran into Joan's bedroom, sat on the bed, and cried. Once the news sank in, we immediately started planning the baby shower. "Wishes Do Come True" was the theme. Ten days later, we found out the baby was a boy. It was a difficult pregnancy on Heather. The baby was fine. She had a cyst on her ovary that caused extreme pain and injured an abdominal muscle. It was going to be a long couple of months.

Was I dreaming, or had it really been five years since the trial ended? Julia was five. She would be starting school in the fall. It seemed so unreal. What had I done for the last five years? It was like a dream. I had started a business, finished school, become a NOVA board member, and become very active in the organization and politics. Not to mention my family was expanding by leaps and bounds. Why did it all seem like a dream? I felt like I was on the ceiling looking down and not really participating in any of the life that was happening. I was a fake, acting the part of a loving mother, grandmother, and friend and feeling nothing.

When the envelope appeared in my mailbox from the state victims' advocate office, it was real. My palms were sweaty and my face, beet red. I was feeling panicked. Jimmy Galione was applying for parole. He had been sentenced to five to ten years. It could not happen. He could not be released. I called my NOVA advocate and asked what we could do to stop his release. Our only recourse was to write letters to the parole board. We were not allowed to appear at any of the meetings. I was scared. I was in no way, shape, or form emotionally ready to even fathom the idea of him free. I hated Judge Heckler. All the feelings I had at the sentencing came flooding back. We all wrote our letters. There was nothing else we could do. We waited.

March brought more baby news. Jill was expecting *again*. The news came just in time to soften the blow of the sixth anniversary of David's death.

Time was beginning to soften the pain around the edges. I was remembering more of the happy memories with my brother and dwelling less on the horror of his death. I still had my moments and could not control the images of *that night* when they snuck up on me out of nowhere. I became angry that David was not there to greet his new nieces and nephews, and yet I was filled with hope at each new life given to our family.

On July 13, 2005, Ryan Andrew Schoell was born. As he took his first breath, I looked up at the beautiful sky and smiled. I thanked God. I felt David's warm smile. He would have been relieved and so happy for Heather. The picture of her holding that healthy newborn will be with me forever.

My brother Frank and his wife, Cheryl, were expecting a baby. This truly was a miracle. I was beaming with joy. I wanted to share this news with David. We all did.

## /////

I was still feeling the joy of this news when the letter arrived from the parole board. Jimmy Galione was going to be released from prison. I was devastated. What was the parole board thinking? Our letters were not good enough? We didn't deserve just a *little* more peace in our lives? Would he get out and kill again and put some other family through the nightmare we were enduring? Would he or his family harass us again? I had so many questions. Would it *finally* be time for the district attorney's office to act on the other arrests? I was quite sure Galione would not cooperate with them. Why would he *ever* do the right thing?

I left it up to my daughter Joan to stay in touch with the police. I could no longer handle the rejection. She was working with the Bristol Borough police now, so I hoped she would be able to get some answers. I hoped she was asking them every day, but I knew that was not the case. If I am known as the quiet one, my Joan is the silent one. I could only hope the thought of her in the police station on a daily basis would remind Randy and, of course, Chief Porter.

It was that day I decided to write this book. I had kept a journal, so I took it out and read each page. I read all of the newspaper articles my daughter, Jill, had kept so meticulously. I acquired the court documents. It was painful and slow going at first, and then the words came. They came in intervals, sometimes pages at a time, and at other times, merely sentences.

I wondered who from our family would be the first to run into Galione. I hoped it would not be my son.

I called his parole officer. I wanted to know the conditions of his release. One of the conditions was that if he were to run into any family member or friend of David, he was to immediately leave.

Of course, it was my son who ran into him first. Why did I know that would be the case? My son was in the Uni-Mart, a small convenience store in Bristol. When Galione saw my son in the store, he turned around and left. At least he did what he was supposed to do. Would it continue?

It was really an awful thing to think, but I almost wished he would hurt someone else so he had to go back to prison. My real self would never wish that pain on another family. I could not control my thoughts. I was just so frustrated with the justice system. People that wrote bad checks to feed their families got longer sentences than this murderer.

I busied myself with NOVA, took all the courses, and did the training I needed to do to be able to help others. I joined the speaker's bureau. The first time I spoke in front of a group, it was excruciating. I could not control my emotions as I told my story, but I got through the speech. The group was kind and invited me back to speak again. It took three speaking engagements before I was able to maintain my composure.

I found something I really liked to do. I enjoyed informing Bucks County Communities of the services NOVA offered and was surprised at how many people had no idea such an organization existed.

I really enjoyed meeting people too. It was so comforting when they would come up to me afterward and say, "I remember that story. I remember your brother." People are innately good. I saw that, and I believed it was true. There were just a few who, with their twisted, broken, bad choices, could shatter the lives of so many.

I was terrified to go anywhere in Bristol alone. I did not want to run into anyone from the Galione or Reeves families. I stuck to visiting homes. I tried to stay out of public places unless I had someone with me. Of course the surge of fear always went through me when I knew I would be speaking. Would one of *them* or their family show up?

In October, my nephew Tony was involved in a car accident. My sister's son was sixteen years old. He and his friends where at football practice and decided afterward to go to Taco Bell. Driving down Route 13 toward Bristol Borough, Tony's friend lost control of the car and crashed into a bridge embankment. The friend was killed instantly. Two others were in critical condition. All I could think as I looked around the hallway in that hospital was, *No, this was not going to happen to us again.* Another one of the boys died. My heart broke for their families. I knew the look in their eyes. I felt their pain.

I was so worried about my sister. If baby Tony (yes, we all called him that ) did not make it through this, my sister would *never, ever* recover. Tony had many injuries, the worst being a broken neck. I was allowed to see him briefly before they transported him to St. Christopher's Hospital for Children in Philadelphia. He was alert and able to talk, which gave me great hope.

He improved quickly and was doing well. His football days were over, and I know that was sad for him. I was so thankful to God that, not only was he alive, he was not paralyzed. I worried about him emotionally. He had just lost two *close* friends.

My sister did not deserve this fear. Tony was only sixteen. These were *good* kids. There had been no alcohol or reckless driving involved. I felt selfish for feeling sorry for Tony and my family when two others where burying their young sons. I refused to become obsessed with dark feelings. It was a long recovery, but Tony would be fine. He had to be.

That fall, I was asked to co-chair NOVA's largest fundraiser of the year. It was so exciting to work on the committee and then see the Galaxy Art Show and Sale come to life on opening night. The show was a success and raised much-needed funds for the agency. I knew why I was involved with the organization, so it was interesting to find out why others were. Some had tragic stories, and others just wanted to help. Why did it take a tragedy for me to want to help? I promised myself I would never allow that to happen again. I would always be involved in something that involved helping my community.

The holidays arrived once again, as they do *every* year. I was getting excited and anticipating the birth of Jill and Kevin's new baby. Another New Year's Eve came and went. As usual, and unfortunately as I expected, no new arrests were made.

My pity party was interrupted this year. On January 11, 2006, Avery Paige Timm entered our family. She was very tiny. Avery had a double hernia that required surgery. When I handed that tiny girl over to a nurse at St. Christopher's Hospital for Children, I nearly passed out. I cried, and Jill cried. I prayed so hard and hoped God wasn't sick of hearing me.

Avery came out of the surgery fine. As far as Jill and I, we will never recover.

Julia turned six. Another year since the trial ended. I was really losing hope. I was just going to be forced to live in a world where murderers were allowed to walk free. My strength to fight was gone. I was angry with myself for not beating down the district attorney's door. I was not putting any pressure on the police. I was thinking of doing all of this and more, but I did nothing.

A letter arrived from the parole board. Jerry Reeves was requesting parole. I wondered if writing a letter even mattered. I decided I had to try. I felt like I had to force my family to write letters. We all wrote them and waited.

Another April arrived. Another ecumenical service was held at the park, and unfortunately, there where many new victims and their families. I tried to think of the positive things in my life. A lot had changed in seven years. A lot happened in our family, and David should have been there. How could I help but be angry?

On May 8, 2006, Baron Von Streibig was born. I was once again blessed to be right there as this new life took his first breath. I felt David's presence in the room. I could hear him whispering, "Spanky, you did it!" He would have loved this day.

# WHAT WAS I THINKING?

I received the news that Jerry Reeves would not be released on parole. My body was shaking as I opened the envelope and read the news. I cried. Then I cried some more.

Of course, this news brought up thoughts of the investigation. Joan told me Randy convinced her the case was still open and being worked. Matt, the prosecutor, had left the area. The rumor was he could not tolerate working with Diane Gibbons. *Who could?* I thought. I just felt like we had no one on our side. *One more year of her,* I thought. *As soon as she is out of that office, I will beg the new district attorney to sign the arrest warrants.* I was not going to waste any more time on her. I did believe in karma though, and she had a bucketful due.

I was working on rebuilding my life. I'd lost eight years and would never get them back. I wasted eight years in a dead-end relationship. I had a lot of time to make up.

I asked my business partner to give me two weeks to get moved and settled into Heather and Matt's house. With my personal problems and a few of my partner's own problems, the business was suffering. I could not wait to get back to it full force without any obstacles from my ex. I also wanted to stay away for the two weeks because I did not want her or her family hassled. She had just had a baby, and I didn't want to take any chances.

I was devastated when the two weeks was up and she told me she had closed the business. No discussion. That phone call crushed me. Was I in for another legal battle? I had no energy for any of that. I was so hurt. I was there for her during her own personal crisis after crisis. I never complained. I did whatever I could for her. She simply wanted me to pay half of the outstanding business debt and be done with the whole thing. Well, without the business, I had no income. I had no idea what I had done to deserve that, but I had no time to deal with her issues. I was sure it was all about money, and that, I felt, was so selfish. That business was what motivated me to remove my feet from the floor I was stuck to. My commitment and belief in that business gave me the courage I needed to give up *everything* I had and move on. I really had *nothing!*

I fought the depression. I would do what I could to start over on my own. I babysat all of my grandkids during the day and did whatever work I could for NOVA at night. The pay was awful, but I was happy.

I was also single again. I joined, with the help of my girls, online dating services and had a great time. If I wasn't watching the kids or working with NOVA, I was dating. I dreamed of starting my own business again, but in the meantime, I was having a great time. I will never be able to properly thank Heather and Matt for their support during that time.

I was thinking a lot about how together my life used to be. I had a house, and I thought I had enough together for a rainy day. I thought I had people in my life I could trust, like a mother. I thought I had security. I had a business partner who I believed was a friend.

When violence struck my family, the effects were paralyzing. I was rendered helpless. I do not think anyone can ever be prepared to lose a loved one, no matter what the circumstances. I now know the meaning of *save for a rainy day*. When financial experts tell you to have enough money in reserve to cover six months of bills and living expenses, believe them. I thought I was doing well. I had the 401k, money in the credit union. I thought I had plenty saved. I felt good about my finances back then. In reality, I may have been prepared for a bit of rain. I spent my May mortgage money in the hospital in four days, just feeding all of us. I was out of work for six weeks after Dave died and another six weeks for the trial. I had medical emergencies and was out of work. I left a relationship. I went through a lawsuit that was expensive and never received the judgment I was awarded. I needed to be prepared for a category-five hurricane. The rain just poured and poured all over, and when it blew out, it took everything with it.

I figured I had plenty of time now to get my financial house back in order. In the meantime, I relished every moment of firsts with Dominic, Morgan, Jimmy, Ryan, and Avery. I spent so much quality time with Kyle, and that was priceless. I was blessed to be able to play my days away and was honestly playing my nights away too.

I had plenty of time alone at night to think. I thought about *that night* often. I had always thought Dave had been coming west on Wilson Avenue. I realized he was driving east. Jerry Reeves's car must have been following him down Route 13, Greene Lane, and then onto Wilson Avenue. I believe Dave pulled over because Jerry was flashing his lights or beeping his horn. David most likely assumed it was someone he knew. Perhaps he thought it was one of my kids or my sister or any one of his many friends. As Jerry walked up to the car and Dave rolled the window down, I know Jerry punched David, and the others in his car surrounded David's car. Joey and Anthony got out of the car. There was a fight that did not last long. Dave, Joey, and Anthony were stunned. As they tried to pull away, they were surrounded. I believe Dave was struck in the back of the head with something as soon as he got out of the car. He stumbled to the driveway, being hit with *something* the whole way. Will I *ever* know the entire truth? I hope so. Will the others be arrested—*ever?* I'm not going to give up—*ever!* There is no statute of limitation on murder.

I wished Galione and Reeves, as well as their families, would turn the other way when they saw us. I wished they would find some shred of compassion.

I thought a lot about Anthony and Joey and Dominic. Anthony and Joey were the last people on earth to hear David. They were the last two to see him as he was when he was alive—a big, strong, gentle giant. I wondered what they were thinking. Did they torture themselves like I did, going over and over *that* night in their minds? Did David ever come to them in their dreams?

I also thought about *my* friends. I was so busy with the babies and my blossoming social life, I never saw or heard from any of them. I really missed Tina. I wondered if I had done something wrong. Was she sick of my sadness and depression? Maybe she had stuff going on in her life and needed me but felt I couldn't be there. That made me sad. Or does life take people in different directions? Of course, there were the friends that turned out to be not worth my time—the ones that said, "Get over it already," and "Move on." I was making some new friends at NOVA, but I really did miss some of the old ones.

I thought about the psychic *that* night at Michael's Café. He clearly saw something violent was going to happen. He told Joan to crawl under the car to be safe. Why didn't Dave crawl under the car? Why did he see Joan and not Dave in the violence?

/////

Statistics show road rage is becoming an increasing problem in our nation. It is bullying with a 2,000-pound weapon. If you find yourself in a harassing situation by another driver, *do not react!* Avoid making any eye contact; this could be a trigger for confrontation. Do not be tempted to accelerate, break, or swerve suddenly. This may also be seen as confrontational and increases your chance of losing control of your vehicle. If a driver continues to hassle you or you think you are being followed, drive to the nearest police station or busy place and get help.

/////

I thought about people like Natalie Holloway's family. They have no idea what happened to their daughter. They have no idea where she is. We may not have all the pieces, but we do know David is dead. We know where his ashes are. These poor parents had no clue. I cried and prayed for them. I saw their fight for justice was going to be agonizing. I wanted to hug them. I wanted to go to Aruba and help them find their baby.

I tried to stop thinking about all of this stuff. I needed to move on and put some kind of life together for myself. I knew without a doubt, I wanted to help victims. That would always be a part of my life. I devoted a lot of time to NOVA. I hoped God had put me on the right path.

I wanted to be in love again one day—really in love. I wanted someone who loved me just the way I was.

I was having a great time in my new dating adventures but rarely went out more than once with one person. I made a list of criteria. They had to have been married before, they had to have children, and, of course, no drug or alcohol problems. That really narrowed the pool, just those simple things. I was not ready for a relationship, so I just decided to have fun. I felt like a teenager for the first time in my life. I married and had children so young. I never had the experience of dating and just going out and having a good time.

There always was this little voice inside of me that reminded me, *You should be sad. How dare you smile? Your brother has been beaten to death.* I would feel guilty and then quickly remind myself that I was alive. David would have wanted me to live my life and find some happiness.

I thought about the people who were helped through David's organ donation. Actually, his organs were unable to be used. They were able to use his eyes and parts of his leg bones. I know they did not use his *actual* eyes, just the retina, but I still find myself searching for those eyes in crowds.

These were all the things my crazy, mixed up mind was thinking about during that time in my life, all those nights I spent alone.

# THE NEVER-ENDING STORY

I was sitting at my computer in my room at Matt and Heather's house trying to write. Kyle was bouncing on my bed. Heather was in and out to check on him. She was always worried that Kyle was bothering me. She was so ridiculous sometimes. I was so in love with that child there was nothing he could *ever* do to bother me. In him I saw an angel, and when angels are close, God cannot be too far behind.

I decided to check my e-mail. I had an e-mail from Singlesnet, one of the dating sites I had joined. I opened the message.

There was this burly-looking man in a wife beater leaning against a motorcycle. *Oh LORD*, I thought. Heather said, "Look at his eyes." I did; he looked like he was staring at me. I also saw pain in his eyes, deep pain. I opened the message. It read, "You like to cook and I like to eat." It was not the most creative but probably honest. I checked out his profile. I answered the e-mail. He lived pretty far away, and that would have normally stopped me right there. Why didn't it stop me?

After talking on the phone a few times, we agreed to meet half-way at Chickie and Pete's on the boulevard in Philadelphia. He called as I was getting close to the restaurant and said Chickie and Pete's was mobbed and asked if we could meet at the Bennigan's next door. I agreed.

I parked my car on the side of the restaurant, got out, and walked around to the front. There he was. He was cute. I immediately liked John; he was soft spoken.

Minutes into our conversation, he mentioned he was a recovering alcoholic. That red flag flew up in my mind. Then he told me he had been sober for sixteen years. *Okay then, that should be okay.* We sat there talking for a long time. He asked me if I would like to take a ride to the seashore. I was a little nervous, but after calling Heather and telling her where we were going, I felt better. On the dashboard of his truck, he had a stuffed Winnie the Pooh. I love Pooh!

During the two-hour ride, we talked about everything. I do not usually talk about David when I first meet someone; it's just a matter of not wanting to make them uncomfortable.

John told me the story of his seventeen-year-old son who had died of suicide. When he told me the date his son died, April 26, my body got hot. It was such a weird feeling. David's actual death date was April 28, but for me, it was always the twenty-sixth. That was the day I heard the doctor tell Randy that David was brain-dead. What a weird coincidence. So we told each other our horror stories.

As we were driving into the New Jersey shore town of Strathmere, off to the left, we saw fireworks. We both thought that was a little strange; it was only May 20, not even Memorial Day yet. We decided to walk down to the beach. I should have been freezing, but I wasn't cold at all. We sat on the beach and looked up at the stars. It sounds goofy, but I had never in my life seen so many big stars. The sky was covered. It was beautiful.

It is hard to explain, but I did not feel like I was in my body that night—that crazy thought of floating through time. As we talked, John told me this was the very spot he'd scattered his son's ashes.

When I think back, I feel that should have been creepy, but it wasn't. It was comforting.

Both of our fathers were named Francis John. That was weird enough, but both fathers lived in Port Orange, Florida. Was it just another strange coincidence? The crazy thing was, I do not believe in coincidences in God's world. I believe everything happens for a reason. I was never more convinced of that theory. I did not just happen to meet this man. Some force greater than us had a hand in putting us together.

As much as I believed that theory, I also knew I was not ready for a relationship. I had a life to put back together. I was also having a great time being single.

Caution to the wind, as they say. The next weekend, Memorial Day weekend, I found myself on the back of John's motorcycle headed to the seashore. I had not been on a motorcycle in over thirty years, and the last time I was, it resulted in a crash. I should have been scared to death, but I was not scared at all. I loved the ride and felt safe. It was chilly, but we made the most of it and had a great weekend. There were a few red flags that popped into my mind, but I quickly shot them down. I knew he was a good man.

I was still a news junkie and was so discouraged that people just did not seem to care what our elected officials were doing. There was so much bickering about the war. There was so much controversy between parties. I asked everyone I knew if they believed there were controversies surrounding 9/11. Everyone told me they believed something wasn't right, but nobody did or said anything. Why that should confuse me was kind of ridiculous; in my own neighborhood, nobody seemed to care there were murderers walking the streets.

I decided to be hopeful about the future. Before long, Diane Gibbons would be out of office and George Bush would be back on his ranch fishing. I would just wait.

Besides, I had a new man in my life, and for a change, my kids seemed to like him. Of course, Jill held out a little; she was convinced everyone was out to axe murder me. I did listen to her, however, because her intuition has always been pretty good.

I remembered taking a trip to Florida with her when she was three, and she laid herself across the doorway of the plane, screaming that the plane was broken. The pilot told me I had to get her on the plane and keep her quiet; she was scaring the other passengers. Well, somewhere over Maryland, the engine fell off our plane. We had to make an emergency landing in Washington. Thank God we were all safe, but I knew Jill had inherited my intuitions.

She used to sit in her crib at our house in Bristol and talk to a friend named Mary. It turned out a Mary had been born and died in our house. At first, I thought she was seeing the blessed mother, the very one I saw when I was pregnant with Jill. I was convinced when Jill kept saying her friend Mary left toys in the closet for her to play with. During some remodeling, we removed a wall in Jill's closet and found a toy box full of old toys. We indeed had the ghost of Mary living in our house.

The holidays were very busy that year. My baby parade had me bursting with love and pride. I had a new love in my life. I met John's son, Michael. I met him at a kickboxing match. It was a nerve-wracking event, since Michael was doing the boxing. Thank God, he won. I liked Michael immediately and had a hard time believing any of the stories John told me about what a terror Michael *used* to be.

The kickboxing thing was hard to get used to. I closed my eyes a lot in the beginning, but before long, I was one of his biggest fans. We were all so proud when he won the title. He has retired and is just coaching now, and I wince a little whenever he talks about defending his title.

Time management was becoming an issue with John and me living so far apart. He asked me to move in with him. I had vowed to myself to never *live* with anyone again. Would I be happy being an hour away from my kids and the babies? I was already not seeing enough of Birna and Michael or any of my friends.

After much deliberation, I decided it was the right move for me. My kids were grown; they would visit me, and I would visit them. I still procrastinated in making the decision. I had to be 100 percent sure I was making the right decision for me and my family. I new John was the right man for me, and there was no doubt I wanted to be with him. I was scared of the change.

It was January 24, 2007, and Julia's seventh birthday. I thought about the last seven years as I drove to John's house. It was a long ride. I was having my usual end-of-the-trial-date-and-no-new-arrests meltdown.

I was sick of feeling guilty over my devastating feelings every year on Julia's birthday. It just was not fair to her. She was a beautiful little girl, and she came along at just the right time. I wanted to celebrate *her* on that date.

When I got to John's house, he greeted me with a big hug. As I usually did in his arms, I felt safe. I noticed a nicely wrapped gift on the dining room table. I assumed I was getting a new biker-girl something. I sat down and opened the box and found another box and then another. When I got to the tiniest box, John put in the CD of our favorite song, "Wave on Wave" by Pat Green, got down on his knee, and proposed. Once the shock wore off, I accepted. On that day, this caring, amazing man changed January 24 for me for-ever. That date would now be the celebration of a beautiful little girl being born into our family just when we needed her and the anni-versary of *our* engagement. The end of the trial was pushed to the bottom of the pile. I felt so blessed to have an amazing man in my life. He listened to me and always seemed to know the right thing to do to make me feel better.

That April, together, we watched videos of David and John (John's son). John attended the ecumenical service at the park with me. We lit candles.

Somehow, the two of us found our way out of the darkness and found each other.

I like to think David and John are friends in heaven and had a hand in putting the two of us together. The two of them were a lot alike. It is a nice thought.

On June 17, 2007, on the beach in Strathmere, New Jersey, the very spot where we had our first date, I married my best friend. Our families were there, some friends, and all of the babies. It seemed to go by so fast, but the memory is one that will last forever.

#### /////

Judge Heckler's wife became a NOVA board member. I felt very uncomfortable but decided to keep my feelings to myself. She had no idea who I was. I decided the mission was about NOVA, not the people involved, and in all fairness, she was not her husband. If I judged her, that would make me no better than the family of the murderers.

That fall, at the Network of Victim Assistance Galaxy Art Show and Sale, I ran into Judge Heckler. I told him I was writing this book and asked him why he gave the sentences he gave. He didn't even look me in the eye when he answered.

"Oh that was a mutual fight," he answered. I walked away full of anger and disappointment. He arrogantly believed he was right in going against the jury's conviction of third-degree murder. He could not have been more wrong! When Judge Heckler was in the state house, he created mandatory sentencing guidelines. But the sentences he imposed were nowhere near his guide. In Pennsylvania, conspiracy carries the same penalty as the murder. They both should have been sentenced to twenty-five to thirty years, based on the chart. The jury was furious, and so am I. Their recommendation was thirty years.

#### /////

On April 29, 2008, my niece Ava Von was born. Once again, I was right there and witnessed her take her first breath. I cannot help but smile when I think of David smiling down from heaven and even laughing as my brother Frank juggles work, a wife, two teenagers, and two babies. I smile every time the thought enters my mind.

/////

In June of 2008, Jerry Reeves was granted parole after serving eight years. The boy who was voted most likely to get in trouble by his 1996 graduating class at Bristol Junior-Senior High School was walking the streets of Bristol again. The police assured us they were keeping an eye on his activity. So far, they have not been, because one of the conditions of his parole was to stay out of Bristol, and *he is in Bristol.*

My family remains deeply fractured, which leads me to believe we were much more dysfunctional than I would have believed prior to David's death. Or perhaps it is because *everyone* grieves so differently. Then again, it could be as simple as life just goes on. We still gather at his tree every April as a family. We still gather at the memorial on Wilson Avenue on April 24 and July 3.

April of 2009 marked the ten-year anniversary of David's death. I actually hate that word *anniversary.* It sounds too much like a celebration. The ecumenical service at Core Creek Park was especially moving. Joey, Anthony, and several more of David's friends attended. Matt, the assistant district attorney who fought so hard for David, is now working in south New Jersey, joined us for the tenth anniversary. That touched me deeply. He has not forgotten David or our family. It is so comforting to me when I realize David has not been forgotten. The weather, which does not always cooperate in April, was just right that evening. We all sat under Dave's tree and remembered him solemnly. We all felt his presence. Ten years sounds like such a long time. An entire decade has passed.

I cannot conjure up a picture in my mind of David at thirty-six. I do try, I just cannot picture him. In my mind, he will forever be twenty-six. I try so hard not to dwell on the *what ifs*—what if he were still here? What would he have named his next child? Where would he be living? Would his band have made it? The fact is, he is not here, and I cannot change that. I am a sister that lost her brother, just another person in a sea of faces with a tragic story to tell.

I like to believe I have gone through the five stages of grief like all the books on the subject instruct. Then again, I wonder if I am still going through them. The impact of grief was not even recognized by the psychological community until the 1980s. When you think about it, grief impacts everyone's life everyday in some way. When your car will not start, for example, that is a definite grief-stricken moment. It can ruin your day. It takes time—time that you cannot get back. When you burn toast, you are feeling a bit of grief. These are simple examples of everyday life, but everyone handles these very simple catastrophes differently. Some simply say, "Oh well," and call the mechanic, while others yell and scream.

Even now, there are only a few studies being done on the correlation between grief and physical illness. I hope the future will bring more studies and more awareness to this problem. I believe without a doubt that I internalized my grief, and it made me physically sick. I thought I was so tough and so smart and knew the five steps that I could go at it alone.

I believe counseling of some sort is a must for anyone who has had a traumatic event impact their lives, most definitely when violence strikes you or someone you love. No one is strong enough to go it alone. I most certainly could not have gone through this darkness without the help of NOVA.

## /////

I am still close with Birna and will be forever. I think she is amazing. She once told me, "I am so young, so if this is the worst thing that ever happens to me, I have something to look forward to." She has worked very hard to make a life for her and Michael. Michael is doing very well in school and *loves* baseball and *music*. I no longer look at Michael and see David. Well, that is not entirely true; the resemblance is amazing, but now I see Michael. He is such a good kid, with his own personality, and I have no doubt he will grow up to be a man we will all be proud to know.

I am so proud of my brother Nick. He is finally spending some quality time with Michael. It was a long time coming, and I'm sure he had his reasons. I am thankful he is there now and pray he continues to be there. I hope my brother Frank and my son soon follow. Michael needs their influence and guidance in his life.

Nick and I are *chatting* again now, and someday I hope we will be close again. I have really been missing him. As far as my mother is concerned, that door is closed and will remain closed until she becomes the Christian woman she claims to be and does the right thing. Even then it will most likely be too late.

Diane Gibbons, the skirt and sneaker wearer, is *finally* no longer the Bucks County district attorney. I wanted to have a party to celebrate. Now she is a judge. What *lucky* criminals we have in Bucks County, Pennsylvania. As soon as the new district attorney is elected, I will be knocking on the door. Judge Heckler resigned. To that, all I can say is *no big loss.*

/////

On May 29, 2009, Adriana Jean was born. Allyson and big brother,Dominic,as well as the rest of us,were overjoyed.

On June 1, 2010, Peyton Elizabeth joined our family. My daughter,Jill, now has three little princesses.

In August of 2010, Jimmy Galione was released from parole. He is now free to come and go as he pleases. I have yet to run into him or Jerry. I hope I never do, but I'm sure it is inevitable. Galione's sister, Angela, continues to lash out at our family.

Judge Heckler is the new Bucks County District Attorney. I am at a loss for words.

In March, Birna walked out of her front door to see Jerry Reeves going through her trash. Again, I have no words.

I will *never* get over David's murder. The pain will always be with me. I just choose to focus more on life now. I still have my very sad moments and actual spasms of overwhelming grief, but now I like to think of them as my body's way of reminding me to be thankful to God every day for *everyone* I am blessed to love in my life and for the glorious memories I have of my baby brother with the blonde hair, playing in the leaves.

Doreen and David, Washington Crossing State Park, 1974. I will always remember the blonde baby playing in the leaves.

# MAYBE TODAY?

Written by me and read at the Nova Ecumenical Service/David's tree dedication:

You convince yourself everything will be okay
But deep down inside, you know: not today.
Everybody is there looking on
You tell yourself you must be strong.
You close your eyes and try to sleep
Off you sink into the deep.
Hoping to wake with this nightmare gone away
But even in sleep, you know: not today.
The angels came and took him to a another place
Then there was a criminal case.
The tears flow a little at a time

The pain is so deep; you are out of your mind.
So many questions and answers don't come
Where, my God, did this evil come from?
Bits and pieces start to fill the page
This all started with a night of rage.
They would stick together until the very end
Do you think they know the meaning of *friend?*
The guards came and took them away,
But you don't feel better? Not even today.
These tears are really burning my eyes
I want the answers to all of my whys
You realize your tears are not the only ones
There are others like you, and a river of tears runs
In this place of survivors, none of us chose to be
But look at us; our river is becoming a sea
We go on and function, the hours turning into days
Our emotions come and go like giant waves
We are all stuck now on this life raft together
The days go on, and nothing changes but the weather.
If we take all of our tears and build an ocean strong
Maybe we can find a place where violence is always wrong.
We could plant some trees and watch them grow together.
Is it possible to create a forest that will live forever?
For all of us, it started with somebody's choice between right and
wrong.
How is it possible that a bad choice has made so many so sad?
We have taken a single tear and turned it into an ocean strong
Surviving is now the place where we all belong
Our ocean will rise up to the clouds, and down will come rain
Do we dare dream it can wash away some of the pain?
Probably not, but it will help the trees we plant with love
As we continue to look for answers from up above.
Reach out to every child and teach them kindness is the only way
And maybe together we can stop the violence, maybe today.

## /////

LORD, make me an instrument of
Your peace; where there is hatred,
Let me sow love; where there is
Injury, pardon; where this is doubt,
Faith; where there is despair,
Hope; where there is darkness, Light;
And where there is sadness, Joy

—St. Francis of Assisi

# e|LIVE

# listen|imagine|view|experience

## AUDIO BOOK DOWNLOAD INCLUDED WITH THIS BOOK!

In your hands you hold a complete digital entertainment package. In addition to the paper version, you receive a free download of the audio version of this book. Simply use the code listed below when visiting our website. Once downloaded to your computer, you can listen to the book through your computer's speakers, burn it to an audio CD or save the file to your portable music device (such as Apple's popular iPod) and listen on the go!

How to get your free audio book digital download:

1. Visit www.tatepublishing.com and click on the e|LIVE logo on the home page.
2. Enter the following coupon code:
   7170-f20e-26f1-c1a1-9f40-33dc-3818-2be8
3. Download the audio book from your e|LIVE digital locker and begin enjoying your new digital entertainment package today!